# Problem S
## Just for the Fun of It! Book Two

Developed and Published by
## AIMS Education Foundation

This book contains materials developed by the AIMS Education Foundation. **AIMS** (**A**ctivities **I**ntegrating **M**athematics and **S**cience) began in 1981 with a grant from the National Science Foundation. The non-profit AIMS Education Foundation publishes hands-on instructional materials that build conceptual understanding. The foundation also sponsors a national program of professional development through which educators may gain expertise in teaching math and science.

Copyright © 2005, 2010 by the AIMS Education Foundation

All rights reserved. No part of this book or associated digital media may be reproduced or transmitted in any form or by any means—including photocopying, taping, or information storage/retrieval systems—except as noted below.

- A person or school purchasing this AIMS publication is hereby granted permission to make up to 200 copies of any portion of it (or the files on the accompanying disc), provided these copies will be used for educational purposes and only at one school site. The files on the accompanying disc may not be altered by any means.

- Workshop or conference presenters may make one copy of any portion of a purchased activity for each participant, with a limit of five activities per workshop or conference session.

- All copies must bear the AIMS Education Foundation copyright information.

AIMS users may purchase unlimited duplication rights for making more than 200 copies, for use at more than one school site, or for use on the Internet. Contact us or visit the AIMS website for complete details.

AIMS Education Foundation
P.O. Box 8120, Fresno, CA 93747-8120 • 888.733.2467 • aimsedu.org

ISBN 978-1-60519-033-4

Printed in the United States of America

# I Hear and I Forget,

# I See and I Remember,

# I Do and I Understand.

### —Chinese Proverb

# Problem Solving: Just for the Fun of It! Book Two

## Table of Contents

Introduction . . . . . . . . . . . . . . . . . . . . . . . . . . . . 5
Suggestions for Using This Book . . . . . . . . . . . . . . 6
Strategy Reference . . . . . . . . . . . . . . . . . . . . . . . 7

Amazing Arithmetic Arrays . . . . . . . . . . . . . . . . . 9
Zip, Zap, Zorp . . . . . . . . . . . . . . . . . . . . . . . . . 25
The Square Challenge . . . . . . . . . . . . . . . . . . . . 33
Lines, Triangles, and Squares, Oh My! . . . . . . . . 41
Set Counting . . . . . . . . . . . . . . . . . . . . . . . . . . 49
Calendar Counts . . . . . . . . . . . . . . . . . . . . . . . 57
Tinkering With Twos . . . . . . . . . . . . . . . . . . . . 63
Making a Difference . . . . . . . . . . . . . . . . . . . . 69
The Nine-Digit Challenge . . . . . . . . . . . . . . . . . 81
Eight-Digit Addition . . . . . . . . . . . . . . . . . . . . 95
Side by Side . . . . . . . . . . . . . . . . . . . . . . . . . 105
Looking for a Liter . . . . . . . . . . . . . . . . . . . . 113
Piecing Together a Paradox . . . . . . . . . . . . . . 121
Clock Palindromes . . . . . . . . . . . . . . . . . . . . 135
Playing With Palindromes . . . . . . . . . . . . . . . 141
Subtraction Palindromes . . . . . . . . . . . . . . . . 149
Palindromic Ponderings . . . . . . . . . . . . . . . . . 159
Tablet Teaser . . . . . . . . . . . . . . . . . . . . . . . . 169
Mind Reader's Magic Cards . . . . . . . . . . . . . . 175
Standing Invitation . . . . . . . . . . . . . . . . . . . . 185
Binary Bemusements . . . . . . . . . . . . . . . . . . . 197

# Introduction

*Problem Solving Just for the Fun of It! Book Two* is the second book in a series of AIMS publications. Like the first book in the series—*Problem Solving Just for the Fun of It!*—this book also contains a wide variety of open-ended, in-depth, mathematical investigations for students in grades four through nine. These investigations were written with three goals in mind:
- to foster positive feelings about mathematics by introducing teachers and students to the fascinating world of recreational mathematics—doing math just for the fun of it;
- to embody the curriculum and evaluation standards from the National Council of Teachers of Mathematics (NCTM); and
- to provide teachers with a wide selection of motivating problem-solving investigations for their students.

The major goal of this publication is to introduce you and your students to the wonderful world of recreational mathematics. This tradition goes back thousands of years. Unfortunately, this long-standing tradition is absent from many modern classrooms. Mathematics in these classrooms may be viewed as necessary and utilitarian, but certainly not enjoyable. However, with the proper care and nurturing, a positive just-for-the-fun-of-it attitude can be kindled in students. The investigations presented here are intended to help this happen in your classroom.

Along with building positive attitudes toward mathematics, every one of the investigations in this book gives students the opportunity to experience, firsthand, four key NCTM standards:
- mathematics as problem solving,
- mathematics as communication,
- mathematics as reasoning, and
- mathematical connections.

In addition, many of the activities also embody other standards such as patterns and functions, number and number relationships, computation and estimation, probability, algebra, and geometry. When doing the investigations in this book, your students will experience and learn mathematics in the true spirit of the NCTM standards.

Each of the investigations is designed so that it can be done as a stand-alone activity with students who have mastered the basic operations of arithmetic. The activities do not need to be done sequentially, but the more difficult and/or involved investigations have been placed later in the book and are not recommended until students have had sufficient experience with open-ended problems. The investigations cover a broad range of topics and include such things as mathematical patterns, paradoxes, and microworlds. Students who actively engage in these investigations will expand their mathematical horizons and improve their problem-solving and divergent-thinking skills.

It is my sincere hope that this book and its investigations will help you and your students embark on a wonderful mathematical journey. As you travel together, you can explore the power and beauty of mathematics while simultaneously experiencing doing math just for the fun of it. Bon voyage!

Dave Youngs

# Some Suggestions for Using This Book

- **Be enthusiastic and show that you enjoy math.**
  If you want students to develop positive attitudes toward mathematics and problem solving, it is critical that you model these same attitudes. If you become excited when students find a new pattern or make some interesting discovery, they will see that you value and enjoy mathematics.

- **Do the problems yourself.**
  You can't teach problem solving effectively unless you become a problem solver. Doing each investigation yourself before assigning it to students not only gives you the chance to apply your own problem-solving strategies, it also gives you a clear idea of what your students are asked to do in the investigation. So please, resist the temptation to read the solutions before you've tried the problems.

- **Emphasize the process as well as the product.**
  Students often have the mistaken idea that the only important thing in math is to get the right answer. Help dispel this notion by valuing the process of problem solving as much as correct answers.

- **Encourage multiple methods of solution and divergent thinking.**
  Every investigation in this book can—and should—be done in multiple ways. Unlike computation, where a single method is often stressed, good problem solving is divergent and open-ended. There is no single "right way" to do any of these problems.

- **Let students make the problem "theirs" by extending it.**
  The majority of the problems presented here can be extended quite easily. While each investigation includes suggested extensions, it is always best if the ideas for extensions come from the students. When students think of interesting questions to explore, they make the problem their own. This is exactly what mathematicians do when they explore new problems.

- **Foster collaboration.**
  Rather than having students work independently, encourage them to collaborate. Since problem solving is a divergent activity, this allows students to learn from each other as they work together on an investigation.

- **Create a classroom problem-solving strategies chart.**
  As students gain experience in solving problems, they begin to use strategies other than guess and check. After your students have gained some experience in problem solving, create a classroom problem-solving strategies chart together that lists these strategies. Add to this chart whenever students discover new strategies. Your chart may include such things as looking for patterns, drawing pictures or diagrams, organizing information in tables and charts, working backwards, doing similar simpler problems, and asking insightful questions.

- **Build persistence.**
  One of the most important characteristics of a good problem solver is persistence. Students who give up too quickly will never become problem solvers—encourage them to keep trying if they don't find an immediate answer.

- **Explore the problems in depth.**
  Many of the investigations in this book lend themselves to in-depth exploration. This type of exploration requires an investment of time, but this investment should prove valuable.

- **Facilitate—don't tell.**
  It may be difficult to do, but try to get students to discover the richness of each problem through their own explorations, not your explanations. This takes practice, but is well worth the effort. For example, a question like, "How might you organize this information to help you solve the problem?" might push students to come up with their own organizational scheme while saying, "Put the numbers in a table according to the following rules…" solves the problem for students and robs them of the chance to find an organizational scheme for themselves.

- **Don't neglect the wrap-up discussions.**
  In many instances the most valuable part of an investigation is the discussion at the end where students share their thoughts, discoveries, methods, and solutions. These sessions provide students with the opportunity to communicate mathematically with their peers and with you. This discussion can help students expand their problem-solving repertoires as they learn how others have approached the problems. Make sure to leave ample time for this important activity.

| Activities \ Strategies | Guess and Check | Use Manipulatives | Look for Patterns | Use Logical Thinking | Write a Number Sentence | Work Backwards | Organize the Information | Wish for an Easier Problem |
|---|---|---|---|---|---|---|---|---|
| Amazing Arithmetic Arrays | | | X | | X | | X | |
| Zip, Zap, Zorp | X | | | X | | | X | |
| The Square Challenge | | X | X | | | | X | X |
| Lines, Triangles, and Squares, Oh My! | | X | X | | | X | X | X |
| Set Counting | | X | | | | | X | |
| Calendar Counts | | | X | | | | X | |
| Tinkering With Twos | X | | | | X | | | |
| Making a Difference | X | X | X | X | | | | |
| The Nine-Digit Challenge | X | X | X | | X | | X | |
| Eight-Digit Addition | X | X | X | | X | | X | |
| Side by Side | | | X | | | | X | |
| Looking for a Liter | | | X | | | | X | |
| Piecing Together a Paradox | | | | X | | | X | |
| Playing With Palindromes | | | X | | | | X | |
| Clock Palindromes | | | | | | | X | |
| Subtraction Palindromes | | | X | | | | X | |
| Palindromic Ponderings | | | X | | | | X | |
| Tablet Teaser | | | X | X | | | | |
| Mind Reader's Magic Cards | | | X | X | | | X | |
| Standing Invitation | | | X | X | | | X | |
| Binary Bemusements | | | X | | | | X | |

# AMAZING ARITHMETIC ARRAYS

**Topic**
Patterns

**Key Question**
How many interesting patterns and other mathematical content can you discover after carefully examining some simple arrays?

**Learning Goals**
Students will:
- study mathematical arrays,
- search for mathematical content and patterns in these arrays,
- create their own arrays, and
- see if the same patterns hold true.

**Guiding Documents**
*Project 2061 Benchmark*
- *Mathematics is the study of many kinds of patterns, including numbers, shapes, and the operations on them. Sometimes patterns are studied because they help to explain how the world works or how to solve practical problems, sometimes because they are interesting in themselves.*

*NCTM Standards 2000\**
- *Describe, extend, and make generalizations about geometric and numeric patterns*
- *Build new mathematical knowledge through problem solving*

**Math**
Number patterns
Problem solving
Algebraic equations, optional

**Integrated Processes**
Observing
Comparing and contrasting
Relating
Generalizing

**Problem-Solving Strategies**
Look for patterns
Organize the information
Write a number sentence

**Materials**
Student pages
Chart paper, optional
Colored pencils or markers, optional

**Background Information**
This investigation has the potential to be a very powerful one if it is explored in depth for some of the sophisticated mathematical content it contains. The array in this activity is actually a mathematical microworld—an environment governed by simple rules and structures. The rule for this microworld is simple: place consecutive numbers or consecutive multiples of numbers (in order) into each row of a square grid from left to right. The resulting arrays are full of mathematical patterns just waiting to be discovered. With older students, explaining why these patterns occur can lead to a deeper understanding of such mathematical concepts as arithmetic means (averages) and multiples. Older students can also generalize some of the patterns they discover as algebraic equations. Although younger students may not reach that level of sophistication, they should still be able to recognize some of the many patterns that are present in the arrays.

**Management**
1. This problem is an open-ended exploration of a mathematical microworld. If your students are new to open-ended problems, you may need to facilitate the initial discoveries by doing the first array together as a class. Skillful questions can lead students to some of the patterns. (What do you notice about the sums of the diagonals? How do these sums relate to the sum of all four numbers? What are the products of the diagonals?)
2. Because it is open-ended, this activity can be done on multiple levels, depending on the mathematical abilities of your students. At the first level, students find as many patterns as they can. At the next level, they can try to explain the reasons for some of these patterns. At the highest level, students can generalize the patterns and come up with algebraic equations for these generalizations.
3. This problem is broken into two parts that can be done on separate days. The first part deals with two-by-two arrays while the second part deals with three-by-three arrays.

JUST FOR THE FUN OF IT! BOOK TWO © 2010 AIMS Education Foundation

4. Because this problem is such a powerful one, you may want to give students chart paper and markers to record some of their most interesting findings for display in the classroom.

**Procedure**
*Part One (Student pages one to four)*
1. Hand out the first student page and make sure the class understands the instructions. *Study the array and list as many interesting patterns and discoveries as you can. Try to find at least 10 things.*
2. Have students work together in small groups to discover as many things about the two-by-two array as possible.
3. After groups have found at least 10 things, have them share their findings in a whole-class session. If students have missed some of the obvious patterns or discoveries (see *Solutions*), use leading questions to help them find these things.
4. Distribute the second student page and have students use what they discovered about the first array to unlock the patterns in these new arrays. Students should also compare and contrast the patterns in these three arrays. From this comparison, students can come up with some generalizations for *all* two-by-two arrays with consecutive numbers.
5. Have students share their findings in a whole-class session. If any obvious patterns have been missed (see *Solutions*), use questions to help students discover them.
6. Give students the third student page, which contains arrays with consecutive multiples of numbers. Have students repeat the process they used on the second page.
7. Hand out the fourth student page and have students choose some other numbers to place in the arrays (either consecutive numbers, consecutive multiples of numbers, or other organized numbers). This page allows students to discover some generalizations about any two-by-two arrays. For example, the sum of the four numbers is two times the sum of the diagonal. After they fill in the arrays and list their discoveries, have students share these in a whole-class sharing time.

*Part Two (Student pages five and six)*
1. Distribute the fifth student page with the three-by-three array. Have students repeat the process of discovering as many patterns as they can in this larger array. Discuss their findings as a class. Use questions to help students see any patterns they miss. (See *Solutions*.)
2. Hand out the final student page and have students fill in the blank arrays with consecutive numbers other than 1-9 or consecutive multiples of numbers. Give students ample time to explore the patterns in the arrays they created and then have them share their findings.
3. As a class, try to come up with some generalizations about the three-by-three arrays. If appropriate, help students turn these generalizations into algebraic equations. For example, in the three-by-three arrays, the sum of all nine numbers is equal to three times the sum of the diagonal. Also, the sum of the numbers is equal to nine times the middle number.

**Connecting Learning**
*Part One*
1. What discoveries did you make about the two-by-two array(s)? (See *Solutions*.)
2. How did the patterns change as you used consecutive multiples as opposed to consecutive numbers? (See *Solutions*.)
3. What numbers did you use to create your own arrays?
4. What things did you discover that were the same as in the original array(s)? ...different? (See *Solutions*.)

*Part Two*
1. What discoveries did you make about the three-by-three array? (See *Solutions*.)
2. What things were the same, or related to, discoveries that you made about the two-by-two array?
3. What things were different?
4. How did the patterns change as you used consecutive multiples as opposed to consecutive numbers? (See *Solutions*.)
5. How can you explain why any of the patterns you found or discoveries you made occur? (See *Solutions*.)
6. What questions do you have after doing this problem?

**Extensions**
Ideally these extensions will come from the students as they ask questions about their discoveries. If not, you can try to direct their thinking in this direction and try to have them come up with some of these questions to explore.
1. Create and study a four-by-four array.
2. Try using numbers that are not consecutive or multiples and see if any patterns exist.
3. Explore arrays that are rectangular.
4. Look at two-by-two and three-by-three arrays on a calendar, 100s chart, or any other organized grid of numbers. (This is an especially powerful extension explored in the AIMS activities *Calendar Capers* [*Problem Solving: Just for the Fun of It!*] and *Charting Numbers* [*AIMS* Vol. 16, No. 2].)

**Solutions**
This is a partial list of discoveries that your students may make about the different arrays. The list is by no means exhaustive, and hopefully your class will discover things not mentioned here.

*Part One*
*There are several simple patterns in the two-by-two arrays with consecutive numbers (student pages one and two). A few of these are listed here.*
1. The rows (horizontal) consist of an odd and an even number while the columns (vertical) consist of two evens or two odds.
2. The smallest number is in the upper left box while the largest number is in the bottom right.
3. When moving left to right and top to bottom, the numbers in the rows go up by one while the numbers in the columns go up by two. Conversely, going right to left and bottom to top, the numbers in the rows decrease by one and the numbers in the columns decrease by two. (This can model subtraction for younger students and integers for older students.)
4. The numbers in the top-left to bottom-right diagonals go up by three while the numbers in the top-right to bottom-left diagonals go up by one. (Or, going in the opposite directions, negative three and negative one, respectively.)

*When the consecutive numbers in these two-by-two arrays are added, many other patterns become apparent. A few of these are listed here.*
1. The sum of all four numbers in the array is equal to the sums of the two rows.
2. The sum of all four numbers in the array is equal to the sums of the two columns.
3. The sum of all four numbers in the array is equal to the sums of the two diagonals.
4. The sums of the diagonals are the same.
5. The above two findings lead to a generalization that the sum of all the numbers in the array is equal to two times the sum of the numbers in either diagonal.
6. The above generalization can be shortened to: sum equals two times diagonal, which can then be written as the algebraic equation: $s = 2d$.

*When the consecutive numbers in these two-by-two arrays are multiplied, other patterns become apparent. A few of these are listed here.*
1. The product of all four numbers in the array is equal to the product of the products of the numbers in the two rows. (1 x 2 x 3 x 4 = 24; 1 x 2 = 2 and 3 x 4 = 12; 2 x 12 = 24)
2. The product of all four numbers in the array is equal to the product of the products of the numbers in the two columns. (1 x 2 x 3 x 4 = 24; 1 x 3 = 3 and 2 x 4 = 8; 3 x 8 = 24)
3. The product of all four numbers in the array is equal to the product of the products of the numbers in the two diagonals. (1 x 2 x 3 x 4 = 24; 1 x 4 = 4 and 2 x 3 = 6; 4 x 6 = 24)

*When the consecutive-number two-by-two arrays are studied side-by-side, additional patterns become apparent. A few of these are listed here.*
1. The sums of the diagonals are always odd. As you can see below, 1 + 4 = 5, 2 + 3 = 5, 2 + 5 = 7, 3 + 4 = 7, etc.

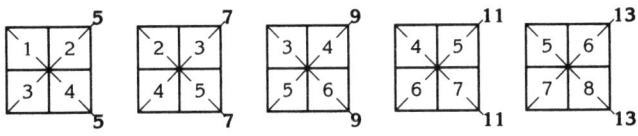

2. As the first number in the array increases by one, the sum of each diagonal increases by two. This can be generalized as follows: if $n$ is the first number in the array, the sum of each diagonal will be $2n + 3$.

**For consecutive numbers**

| First # in array | Sum of diagonal |
|---|---|
| 1 | 5 |
| 2 | 7 |
| 3 | 9 |
| 4 | 11 |
| $n$ | $2n + 3$ |

3. As the first number in the array increases by one, the sum of all the numbers in the array increases by four. This can be generalized as follows: if $n$ is the first number in the array, the sum of all of the numbers in the array is $4n + 6$.

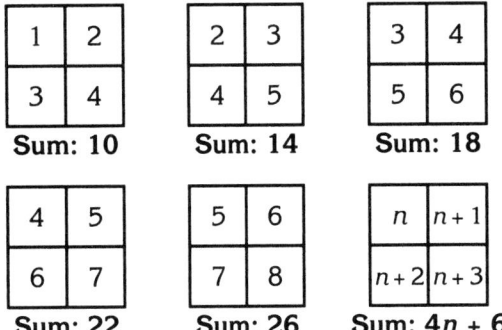

4. When the patterns already mentioned are considered together, the trends become clear.

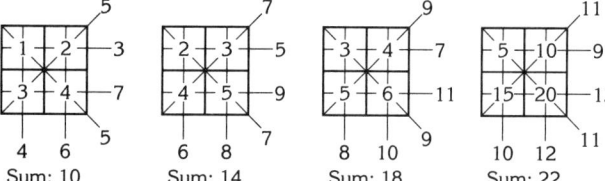

- The sums of the horizontal rows are always odd, and increase by two as the first number in the array increases by one.
  (1 + 2 = 3, 2 + 3 = 5, 3 + 4 = 7, etc.)
- The difference between the sums of the horizontal rows within an array is always four.
  (7 − 3 = 4, 9 − 5 = 4, 11 − 7 = 4, 13 − 9 = 4, etc.)
- The sums of the vertical columns are always even, and increase by two as the first number in the array increases by one.
  (1 + 3 = 4, 2 + 4 = 6, 3 + 5 = 8, etc.)
- The difference between the sums of the vertical columns within an array is always two.
  (6 − 4 = 2, 8 − 6 = 2, 10 − 8 = 2, 12 − 10 = 2, etc.)
- The sums of the diagonals are always odd, and increase by two as the first number in the array increases by one.
  (1 + 4 = 5, 2 + 5 = 7, 3 + 6 = 9, etc.)
- The sums of all the numbers in the array are always even, and increase by four as the first number in the array increases by one.
  (1 + 2 + 3 + 4 = 10, 2 + 3 + 4 + 5 = 14, 14 − 10 = 4, etc.)

*There are a number of different patterns in the two-by-two arrays with consecutive multiples (student page three). A few of these are listed here.*

1. The sums of the diagonals when the numbers in the array are consecutive multiples alternate between odd and even, as shown below.

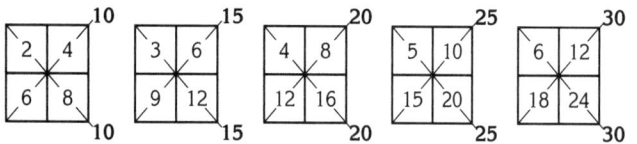

2. When the numbers in the array are consecutive multiples, as the first number increases by one, the sum of each diagonal increases by five. This can be generalized as follows: if the first number in the array is $n$, the sum of each diagonal is $5n$.

**For consecutive multiples**

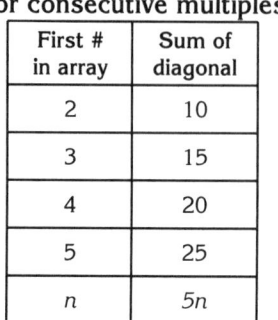

| First # in array | Sum of diagonal |
|---|---|
| 2 | 10 |
| 3 | 15 |
| 4 | 20 |
| 5 | 25 |
| $n$ | $5n$ |

3. When the numbers in the array are consecutive multiples, as the first number increases by one, the sum of all the numbers in the array increases by 10.

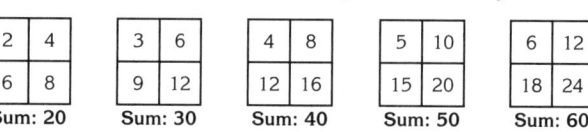

4. When all of the aforementioned patterns are examined together, the trends are, once again, quite clear.

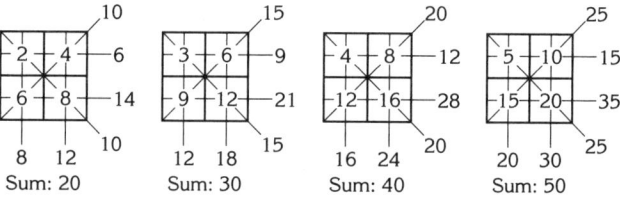

For two-by-two arrays that consist of consecutive multiples:
- The sums of the horizontal rows are even when the first number in the array is even and odd when the first number in the array is odd. The sums of the top rows increase by three as the first number in the array increases by one, while the sums of the bottom rows increase by seven as the first number in the array increases by one. (2 + 4 = 6, 3 + 6 = 9, 9 − 6 = 3, etc. 6 + 8 = 14, 9 + 12 = 21, 21 − 14 = 7, etc.)
- The sums of the vertical columns are always even. The sums of the left columns increase by four as the first number in the array increases by one, while the sums of the right columns increase by six as the first number in the array increases by one. (2 + 6 = 8, 3 + 9 = 12, 12 − 8 = 4, etc. 4 + 8 = 12, 6 + 12 = 18, 18 − 12 = 6, etc.)
- As the first number in the array increases by one, the difference between the sums of the vertical columns increases by two. For example, the difference between eight and 12 is four, the difference between 12 and 18 is six, the difference between 16 and 24 is eight, and so on.
- As the first number in the array increases by one, the difference between the sums of the horizontal rows increases by four. For example, the difference between six and 14 is eight, the difference between nine and 21 is 12, the difference between 12 and 28 is 16, and so on.
- The sums of the diagonals are even when the first number in the array is even and odd when the first number in the array is odd. The sums increase by five as the first number in the array increases by one. (2 + 8 = 10, 3 + 12 = 15, 15 − 10 = 5, etc.)
- The sums of all the numbers in the array are always even, and increase by 10 as the first number in the array increases by one. (2 + 4 + 6 + 8 = 20, 3 + 6 + 9 + 12 = 30, etc.)

*Part Two*
*Patterns in the first three-by-three array:*

1. The sum of all the numbers in the array (one to nine) is 45. Interestingly, this sum can be found by multiplying the middle number (five) by the number of squares in the grid (nine). This total can also be found by multiplying the sum of either diagonal, the middle row, or middle column (15) by three. These generalizations work for *any* three-by-three array and can be turned into algebraic equations ($s = 3d$ and $s = 9m$ where $s$ is the sum of all the numbers, $d$ is the sum of the numbers in either diagonal, and $m$ is the value of the middle number).

| 1 | 2 | 3 |
|---|---|---|
| 4 | 5 | 6 |
| 7 | 8 | 9 |

$1 + 2 + 3 + 4 + 5 + 6 + 7 + 8 + 9 = 45$
$1 + 5 + 9 = 15, 3 + 5 + 7 = 15,$
$2 + 5 + 8 = 15, 4 + 5 + 6 = 15$
$5 \times 9 = 45, 15 \times 3 = 45$

2. The opposite corners of the array (1, 9; 3, 7) add up to 10. Likewise, the numbers in the middles of the opposite sides (2, 8; 6, 4) have sums of 10.

3. When adding the numbers in the horizontal rows, the sums are six, 15, and 24. These are products of three and the middle column numbers: two, five, and eight. The difference between the sums of the horizontal rows is nine.

| 1 | 2 | 3 |
|---|---|---|
| 4 | 5 | 6 |
| 7 | 8 | 9 |

$1 + 2 + 3 = 6 \quad 2 \times 3 = 6$
$4 + 5 + 6 = 15 \quad 5 \times 3 = 15$
$7 + 8 + 9 = 24 \quad 8 \times 3 = 24$
$15 - 6 = \mathbf{9}$
$24 - 15 = \mathbf{9}$

4. When adding the numbers in the vertical columns, the sums are 12, 15, and 18. These are products of three and the middle row numbers: four, five, and six. The difference between the sums of the vertical columns is three.

| 1 | 2 | 3 |
|---|---|---|
| 4 | 5 | 6 |
| 7 | 8 | 9 |

$1 + 4 + 7 = 12 \quad 4 \times 3 = 12$
$2 + 5 + 8 = 15 \quad 5 \times 3 = 15$
$3 + 6 + 9 = 18 \quad 6 \times 3 = 18$
$15 - 12 = \mathbf{3}$
$18 - 15 = \mathbf{3}$

5. The numbers in the middle of each row and the middle of each column are the averages of their respective rows or columns.

| 1 | 2 | 3 |
|---|---|---|
| 4 | 5 | 6 |
| 7 | 8 | 9 |

$1 + 2 + 3 = 6 \quad 6 \div 3 = \mathbf{2}$
$4 + 5 + 6 = 15 \quad 15 \div 3 = \mathbf{5}$
$7 + 8 + 9 = 24 \quad 24 \div 3 = \mathbf{8}$

$\begin{array}{r} 1 \quad 2 \quad 3 \\ 4 \quad 5 \quad 6 \\ +7 \; +8 \; +9 \\ \hline 12 \; 15 \; 18 \end{array}$ $\quad 12 \div 3 = \mathbf{4}$
$\quad 15 \div 3 = \mathbf{5}$
$\quad 18 \div 3 = \mathbf{6}$

6. When the numbers in the array are consecutive, as the first number in the array increases by one, the sums of the diagonals increase by three. This can be generalized as follows: if $n$ is the first number in the array, the sum of each diagonal will be $3(n + 4)$.

**For consecutive numbers**

| First # in array | Sum of diagonal |
|---|---|
| 1 | 15 |
| 2 | 18 |
| 3 | 21 |
| 4 | 24 |
| $n$ | $3(n + 4)$ |

7. When the numbers in the array are consecutive multiples, as the first number in the array increases by one, the sum of each diagonal increases by 15. This can be generalized as follows: if $n$ is the first number in the array, the sum of each diagonal will be $15n$.

**For consecutive multiples**

| First # in array | Sum of diagonal |
|---|---|
| 2 | 30 |
| 3 | 45 |
| 4 | 60 |
| 5 | 75 |
| $n$ | $15n$ |

8. When the patterns in the three-by-three arrays consisting of consecutive numbers are examined together, the trends are very similar to those seen in the two-by-two arrays.

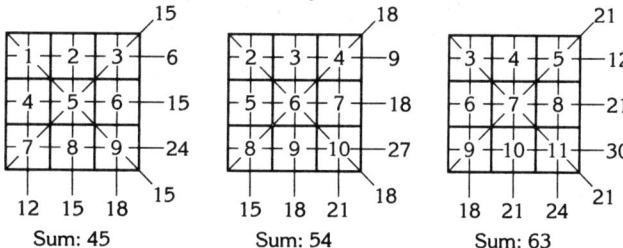

For three-by-three arrays that consist of consecutive numbers:
- As the first number in the array increases by one, the sum of each of the horizontal rows increases by three.
  (1 + 2 + 3 = 6, 2 + 3 + 4 = 9, etc.)
- The difference between the sums of the horizontal rows within an array is always nine.
  (15 – 6 = 9, 24 – 15 = 9, 18 – 9 = 9, 27 – 18 = 9, etc.)
- As the first number in the array increases by one, the sum of each of the vertical columns increases by three.
  (1 + 4 + 7 = 12, 2 + 5 + 8 = 15, 3 + 6 + 9 = 18, etc.)
- The difference between the sums of the vertical columns within an array is always three.
  (15 – 12 = 3, 18 – 15 = 3, 21 – 18 = 3, etc.)
- As the first number in the array increases by one, the sum of each diagonal increases by three.
  (1 + 5 + 9 = 15, 2 + 6 + 10 = 18, etc.)
- As the first number in the array increases by one, the sum of all the numbers in the array increases by nine.
  (45 + 9 = 54, 54 + 9 = 63)

9. The patterns in arrays with consecutive multiples are somewhat more complex than those in arrays with consecutive numbers.

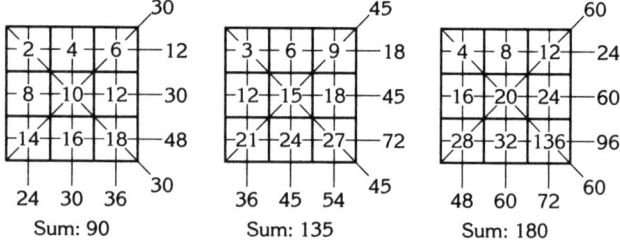

For three-by-three arrays that consist of consecutive multiples:
- The difference between the sums of the horizontal rows within one array increases by nine as the first number in the array increases by one. For example, in the array beginning with two, 30 – 12 = 18 and 48 – 30 = 18. In the array beginning with three, 45 – 18 = 27 and 72 – 45 = 27. The difference between 27 and 18 is nine.
- The difference between the sums of the vertical columns within one array is three times the first number in that array. For example, in the array beginning with two, 30 – 24 = 6, 36 – 30 = 6, 2 x 3 = 6.
- As the first number in the array increases by one, the sum of the top horizontal row increases by six.
  (2 + 4 + 6 = 12, 3 + 6 + 9 = 18, etc.)
- As the first number in the array increases by one, the sum of the middle horizontal row and the middle vertical column both increase by 15.
  (4 + 10 + 16 = 30, 6 + 15 + 24 = 45, etc.)
- As the first number in the array increases by one, the sum of the bottom horizontal row increases by 24.
  (14 + 16 + 18 = 48, 21 + 24 + 27 = 72, etc.)
- As the first number in the array increases by one, the sum of the left vertical column increases by 12.
  (2 + 8 + 14 = 24, 3 + 12 + 21 = 36, etc.)
- As the first number in the array increases by one, the sum of the right vertical column increases by 18.
  (6 + 12 + 18 = 36, 9 + 18 + 27 = 54, etc.)
- As the first number in the array increases by one, the sum of all the numbers in the array increases by 45.
  (90 + 45 = 135, 135 + 45 = 180)

\* Reprinted with permission from *Principles and Standards for School Mathematics*, 2000 by the National Council of Teachers of Mathematics. All rights reserved.

# AMAZING ARITHMETIC ARRAYS

### Key Question

How many interesting patterns and other mathematical content can you discover after carefully examining some simple arrays?

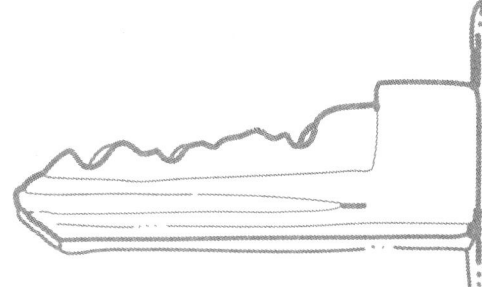

## Learning Goals

### Students will:

- study mathematical arrays,
- search for mathematical content and patterns in these arrays,
- create their own arrays, and
- see if the same patterns hold true.

# AMAZING ARITHMETIC ARRAYS

| 1 | 2 |
|---|---|
| 3 | 4 |

Study the array shown here. See how many interesting things you can discover about this array. Try to find at least 10 things.

Describe all of the patterns and discoveries you make in the space below.

# AMAZING ARITHMETIC ARRAYS

| 2 | 3 |
|---|---|
| 4 | 5 |

| 3 | 4 |
|---|---|
| 5 | 6 |

| 4 | 5 |
|---|---|
| 6 | 7 |

Study the three arrays above. Use what you learned on the first page to help you find as many interesting things as you can about each of these arrays. In addition, note the similarities and differences among these arrays.

JUST FOR THE FUN OF IT! BOOK TWO

# AMAZING ARITHMETIC ARRAYS

| 2 | 4 |
|---|---|
| 6 | 8 |

| 3 | 6 |
|---|---|
| 9 | 12 |

| 4 | 8 |
|---|---|
| 12 | 16 |

Study the three arrays above and list as many patterns and discoveries as you can. Be sure to compare and contrast these arrays with the arrays on the first two pages.

JUST FOR THE FUN OF IT! BOOK TWO © 2010 AIMS Education Foundation

# AMAZING ARITHMETIC ARRAYS

Fill in the blank arrays below with consecutive numbers and/or consecutive multiples of numbers.

Study these arrays and list any additional discoveries that you make.

# AMAZING ARITHMETIC ARRAYS

| 1 | 2 | 3 |
|---|---|---|
| 4 | 5 | 6 |
| 7 | 8 | 9 |

Study the array shown here. See how many interesting things you can discover about this array.

Describe all of the discoveries you make in the space below.

# AMAZING ARITHMETIC ARRAYS

Fill in the blank arrays below with consecutive numbers and/or consecutive multiples of numbers.

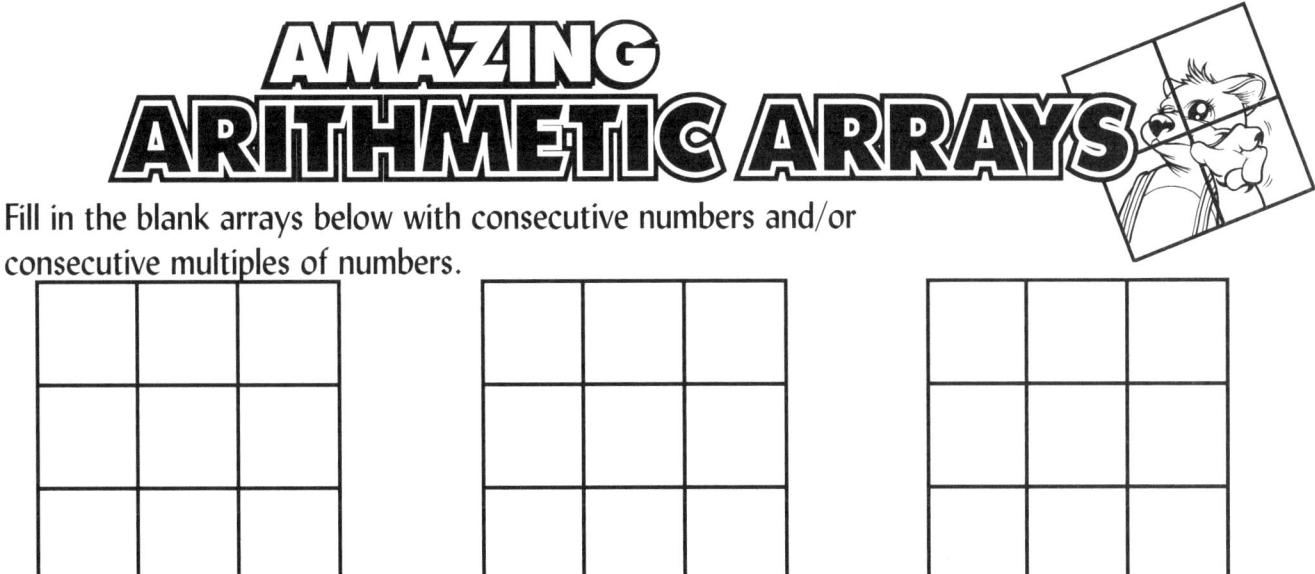

Study these arrays and list any additional discoveries that you make.

# Amazing Arithmetic Arrays

## Connecting Learning

*Part One*

1. What discoveries did you make about the two-by-two array(s)?

2. How did the patterns change as you used consecutive multiples as opposed to consecutive numbers?

3. What numbers did you use to create your own arrays?

4. What things did you discover that were the same as in the original array(s)? ...different?

# Connecting Learning

*Part Two*

1. What discoveries did you make about the three-by-three array?

2. What things were the same, or related to, discoveries that you made about the two-by-two array?

3. What things were different?

4. How did the patterns change as you used consecutive multiples as opposed to consecutive numbers?

5. Can you explain why any of the patterns you found or discoveries you made occur?

6. What questions do you have after doing this problem?

## Topic
Logic

## Key Question
How can you guess the number your partner is thinking of in the fewest tries based on clues that he/she gives you?

## Learning Goal
Students will use logical reasoning and strategy to guess the numbers chosen by their partners in the fewest tries possible.

## Guiding Document
*NCTM Standard 2000\**
- Apply and adapt a variety of appropriate strategies to solve problems

## Math
Logic
Reasoning
Strategy
Problem solving

## Integrated Processes
Observing
Collecting and recording data
Applying

## Problem-Solving Strategies
Use logical thinking
Organize the information
Guess and check

## Materials
Student pages

## Background Information
This activity is a simplified version of a logic game that has been around for a number of years. The original game, called *Pico, Fermi, Bagels*, can be found in *Math for Smarty Pants* by Marilyn Burns and in *The Family Math Book* from the Lawrence Hall of Science. In the simplified version presented here, students are challenged to use logical reasoning to determine which two-digit numbers their partners have picked. Each time they make a guess, their partners give them a clue. The clues provide them with the following information: none of the digits are correct (*Zip*), one of the digits is correct, and is in the right place (*Zap*), or one of the digits is correct, but in the wrong place (*Zorp*). This game helps develop students' logical thinking skills as they try various strategies to find their partners' numbers in the fewest tries possible.

## Management
1. Before students play this game with a partner, it is advisable to play several rounds as a class to familiarize students with the rules and strategy. During these games, you choose a number and give students clues as they make their guesses. A blackline master of the rules has been included that can be displayed using a projection device. This page helps remind the students (and you) what each clue means.
2. This activity has several levels of difficulty. It is fairly simple as presented, but once students grasp the concept, the level of difficulty can be increased by allowing repeating digits, and/or by increasing the number of digits.

## Procedure
1. Introduce the game by explaining the rules and then playing several rounds as a class. *I am thinking of a two-digit number with no repeating digits. When you make a guess about my number, I will give you a clue. Zip means that none of the digits you guessed are correct. Zap means that one of the digits is correct, and is in the right place. Zorp means that one digit is correct, but is in the wrong place. The game is over when you hear me say, "Zap, Zap," meaning that you have both digits correct and in their proper places.*
2. Once you have played enough rounds for students to become comfortable with the game, divide them into pairs. Hand out the student pages and explain that they will take turns picking a number and guessing. The person picking the number records this number on the back of the student page, out of sight of the person guessing. The person guessing then uses the front of his or her own student page to record the numbers guessed and the clues.

3. Allow pairs sufficient time to play several rounds. Encourage them to develop a strategy for guessing the number in the fewest possible tries.
4. If desired, have students try a more difficult version of the problem (see *Extensions*).
5. Close the activity with a time of class discussion where students share the various strategies they developed as they played the game.

**Connecting Learning**
1. What strategy did you develop to determine your partner's number?
2. Did this strategy work every time? Why or why not?
3. How did your strategy change when the numbers could have repeating digits?
4. How did your strategy change when the number of digits was increased?

**Extensions**
1. Allow repeating digits.
2. Play the game with three- or four-digit numbers.
3. Challenge older students to determine the minimum number of guesses needed to win each level of the game (two-digits, two-digits with repeating numbers allowed, three-digits, etc.).

**Solutions**
Since every game of *Zip, Zap, Zorp* is different, it is not possible to provide a solution. Instead, a sample round is outlined below.

Two students—Janet and Carlos—are playing the game. Janet is thinking of the number 29. Carlos is guessing.
Carlos: 37.
Janet: Zip.
*Carlos writes down 37 on his student page along with the clue zip. He knows that neither three nor seven will be in Janet's number.*
Carlos: 48.
Janet: Zip.
*Carlos records the information from this guess on his student page as well. He now knows that four and eight are also not in Janet's number.*
Carlos: 91.
Janet: Zorp.
*As Carlos records this clue, he knows that either a nine or a one is in Janet's number. He decides to go with the nine and see if he is right.*
Carlos: 59.
Janet: Zap.
*Now Carlos knows that either the five or the nine is in the right place, and he is pretty sure that it's the nine. He tests this theory.*
Carlos: 69.
Janet: Zap.
*Now Carlos knows for sure that the nine is in the right place. (If the Zap were for the six and not the nine, this would contradict the Zap given for the previous guess of 59. In that case, if the nine hadn't been correct then the five would have been, eliminating the six in this guess.) Since he now knows the nine is correct and has eliminated all the other numbers except two, he makes his final guess.*
Carlos: 29.
Janet: Zap, zap! Good job, now it's my turn to guess your number.

\* Reprinted with permission from *Principles and Standards for School Mathematics*, 2000 by the National Council of Teachers of Mathematics. All rights reserved.

## Key Question

How can you guess the number your partner is thinking of in the fewest tries based on clues that he/she gives you?

## Learning Goal

### Students will:

use logical reasoning and strategy to guess the numbers chosen by their partners in the fewest tries possible.

I am thinking of a two-digit number with no repeating digits. Try to guess the number. After each guess I will give you one of the following clues:

**ZIP:** No digit is correct.

**ZAP:** One digit is correct, and it is in the right place.

**ZORP:** One digit is correct, but it is in the wrong place.

When you hear me say "Zap, Zap" the round is over—you have guessed both digits correctly and they are in the right place.

# ZIP, ZAP, ZORP

This number guessing game is played in pairs. One person picks a number (starting with a two-digit number with no repeating digits) and the other person tries to guess that number. For each guess, one or more of the following clues is given:

**ZIP:** No digit is correct.

**ZAP:** One digit is correct, and it is in the right place.

**ZORP:** One digit is correct, but it is in the wrong place.

The person guessing writes down each guess and the clue(s) given using the chart on the next page. After the number is found, players switch roles.

Play several rounds. Try to develop strategies to help you find the other person's number using the fewest guesses. List some of these strategies.

Apply these strategies to the next level of play: guessing three-digit numbers. For a greater challenge, allow repeated digits, or try four-digit numbers.

Use the space below to list some of the things you learned while playing this game.

Use the spaces below to help you as you try to guess your partner's number. At the end of each round, record the total number of guesses it took you. See if you can guess your partner's number in fewer guesses than your partner takes to guess your number. (If you run out of space, you can use the back of this paper.)

| Number Guessed | Clue(s) | Number Guessed | Clue(s) | Number Guessed | Clue(s) |
|---|---|---|---|---|---|
| | | | | | |

Total # of guesses: _____   Total # of guesses: _____   Total # of guesses: _____

| Number Guessed | Clue(s) | Number Guessed | Clue(s) | Number Guessed | Clue(s) |
|---|---|---|---|---|---|
| | | | | | |

Total # of guesses: _____   Total # of guesses: _____   Total # of guesses: _____

## Connecting Learning

1. What strategy did you develop to determine your partner's number?

2. Did this strategy work every time? Why or why not?

3. How did your strategy change when the numbers could have repeating digits?

4. How did your strategy change when the number of digits was increased?

# The Square Challenge

## Topic
Problem solving

## Key Question
How many squares of all sizes are there on a checkerboard?

## Learning Goals
Students will:
- use problem-solving methods to find the number of squares of all sizes that exist in a six-by-six grid, and
- use this information to determine how many squares there are on an eight-by-eight checkerboard.

## Guiding Document
*NCTM Standards 2000\**
- *Describe, extend, and make generalizations about geometric and numeric patterns*
- *Build new mathematical knowledge through problem solving*

## Math
Counting
Math patterns
Square numbers
Problem solving

## Integrated Processes
Observing
Collecting and recording data
Generalizing

## Problem-Solving Strategies
Wish for an easier problem
Organize the information
    make a list
Look for patterns
Use manipulatives, optional

## Materials
Student pages
Cut-out squares, optional  (see *Management 1*)

## Background Information
Problem solving is a vital skill for students to develop in order to succeed in all areas of life. This activity requires students to use a basic, but essential, form of mathematical problem solving as they determine the number of squares (of all sizes) that exist in a six-by-six grid. Once they have done this, students will apply these same problem-solving techniques to a more difficult problem (determining the total number of squares in a checkerboard). This strategy of "wishing for an easier problem" to solve a more difficult one is at the core of problem solving, and will serve students well in the future. In addition to the problem solving in this activity, there are many patterns they will encounter as they search for the solutions. Some of these patterns may be applied to help students find the correct answer without actually counting all of the squares.

## Management
1. Some students may have a hard time counting all the squares in the grid. Since the two-by-two through the five-by-five squares can overlap on the grid, this makes it difficult to count them accurately. The squares provided can be cut for students to use as manipulatives. These cut-out squares can be moved around on the grid as an aid to counting.
2. This activity can be done in either an open-ended or a more structured format. For the open-ended approach, give students just the first student page. This page poses the problem and leaves students to solve it any way they wish. For students who need more structure, hand out the second student page in addition to the first. This page provides students with some guidance as they work on this problem.
3. You may wish to display the first student page using a projection device to help you introduce the activity.

## Procedure
1. Hand out the student page(s) and go over the instructions. *Count the number of squares in the grid. Make sure you count squares of all sizes. Use the information you discover to help you find out how many squares of all sizes there would be on a checkerboard, which is eight squares by eight squares.* Be sure that students understand the concept of squares of all sizes.
2. Have students work in small groups to count the squares in the grid and then determine how many would be in a checkerboard.
3. Close with a time of class discussion where students share their answers as well as the problem-solving methods they used to count the squares.

JUST FOR THE FUN OF IT! BOOK TWO

## Connecting Learning

1. How many different sizes of squares are there in the grid? [Six—1 x 1, 2 x 2, 3 x 3, 4 x 4, 5 x 5, 6 x 6]
2. How many squares of each size are there in the grid? (See *Solutions*.)
3. What patterns do you see in these numbers? [They are the square numbers: 1, 4, 9, 16, 25, 36.]
4. How many squares of all sizes are there in the grid? [91]
5. What methods did you use to count the squares?
6. How do you know that you counted all of the squares?
7. How many squares of all sizes are there in a checkerboard? [204]
8. How did you determine this value?

## Extensions

1. Have students count all of the different shaped rectangles that exist in the six-by-six grid (1 x 2, 1 x 3, 2 x 4, 2 x 5, 3 x 6, etc.).
2. Explore the patterns that are found in the number of rectangles that exist in the grid. (See *Solutions*.)
3. Challenge students to develop their own irregular shapes and count how many times they occur in the grid.

## Solutions

The solutions for a six-by-six grid, an eight-by-eight grid, some of the patterns present in the solutions, and the solutions to the first two extensions are given here.

1. For a six-by-six grid, there are 91 squares of all sizes, as shown in the table below. The numbers of squares for the different sizes are the square numbers from one to 36.

**Six-by-six grid**

| Size of square | # of squares |
|---|---|
| 1 x 1 | 36 ($6^2$) |
| 2 x 2 | 25 ($5^2$) |
| 3 x 3 | 16 ($4^2$) |
| 4 x 4 | 9 ($3^2$) |
| 5 x 5 | 4 ($2^2$) |
| 6 x 6 | 1 ($1^2$) |
| Total | 91 |

2. The total number of squares in a checkerboard (eight-by-eight) is 204. As you can see, this answer is easily obtained by applying the pattern that emerged from the six-by-six grid.

**Eight-by-eight grid**

| Size of square | # of squares |
|---|---|
| 1 x 1 | 64 ($8^2$) |
| 2 x 2 | 49 ($7^2$) |
| 3 x 3 | 36 ($6^2$) |
| 4 x 4 | 25 ($5^2$) |
| 5 x 5 | 16 ($4^2$) |
| 6 x 6 | 9 ($3^2$) |
| 7 x 7 | 4 ($2^2$) |
| 8 x 8 | 1 ($1^2$) |
| Total | 204 |

*Solutions for Extensions #1 and #2*

When counting the rectangles in a six-by-six grid, some interesting patterns can be seen. These patterns are shown in the tables that follow and then discussed.

*Rectangles with lengths of one*

| Size of rectangle | # of rectangles | # as a product |
|---|---|---|
| 1 x 2 | 30 | 5 x 6 |
| 1 x 3 | 24 | 4 x 6 |
| 1 x 4 | 18 | 3 x 6 |
| 1 x 5 | 12 | 2 x 6 |
| 1 x 6 | 6 | 1 x 6 |
| **Subtotal** | **90** | **15 x 6** |

*Rectangles with lengths of two*

| 2 x 1 | 30 | 6 x 5 |
|---|---|---|
| 2 x 3 | 20 | 4 x 5 |
| 2 x 4 | 15 | 3 x 5 |
| 2 x 5 | 10 | 2 x 5 |
| 2 x 6 | 5 | 1 x 5 |
| **Subtotal** | **80** | **16 x 5** |

*Rectangles with lengths of three*

| 3 x 1 | 24 | 6 x 4 |
|---|---|---|
| 3 x 2 | 20 | 5 x 4 |
| 3 x 4 | 12 | 3 x 4 |
| 3 x 5 | 8 | 2 x 4 |
| 3 x 6 | 4 | 1 x 4 |
| **Subtotal** | **68** | **17 x 4** |

*Rectangles with lengths of four*

| 4 x 1 | 18 | 6 x 3 |
|---|---|---|
| 4 x 2 | 15 | 5 x 3 |
| 4 x 3 | 12 | 4 x 3 |
| 4 x 5 | 6 | 2 x 3 |
| 4 x 6 | 3 | 1 x 3 |
| **Subtotal** | **54** | **18 x 3** |

*Rectangles with lengths of five*

| 5 x 1 | 12 | 6 x 2 |
|---|---|---|
| 5 x 2 | 10 | 5 x 2 |
| 5 x 3 | 8 | 4 x 2 |
| 5 x 4 | 6 | 3 x 2 |
| 5 x 6 | 2 | 1 x 2 |
| **Subtotal** | **38** | **19 x 2** |

*Rectangles with lengths of six*

| 6 x 1 | 6 | 6 x 1 |
|---|---|---|
| 6 x 2 | 5 | 5 x 1 |
| 6 x 3 | 4 | 4 x 1 |
| 6 x 4 | 3 | 3 x 1 |
| 6 x 5 | 2 | 2 x 1 |
| **Subtotal** | **20** | **20 x 1** |
| **Total** | **350** | |

- The differences between the subtotals increase by two as the lengths increase by one. For example, 90 – 80 = 10, 80 – 68 = 12, 68 – 54 = 14 and so on.
- Each rectangle has an "opposite" that occurs the same number of times. For example, 2 x 4 rectangles and 4 x 2 rectangles each occur 15 times.
- Rectangles that have lengths of one unit all occur in amounts that are divisible by six. In other words, the number of rectangles with sides of one are the products of six and the numbers from one to five.
- This pattern continues with the remaining rectangles, with the product decreasing by one as the side increases by one. Rectangles that have lengths of two units all occur in amounts that are divisible by five. Rectangles with sides of three occur in numbers divisible by four. Rectangles with sides of four occur in numbers divisible by three. Rectangles with sides of five occur in numbers divisible by two. Rectangles with lengths of six occur in numbers divisible by one.

\* Reprinted with permission from *Principles and Standards for School Mathematics*, 2000 by the National Council of Teachers of Mathematics. All rights reserved.

# The Square Challenge

## Key Question

How many squares of all sizes are there on a checkerboard?

## Learning Goals

### Students will:

- use problem-solving methods to find the number of squares of all sizes that exist in a six-by-six grid, and

- use this information to determine how many squares there are on an eight-by-eight checkerboard.

# The Square Challenge

How many squares are there in the grid pictured here? Make sure you count squares of all sizes. Record your answer below.

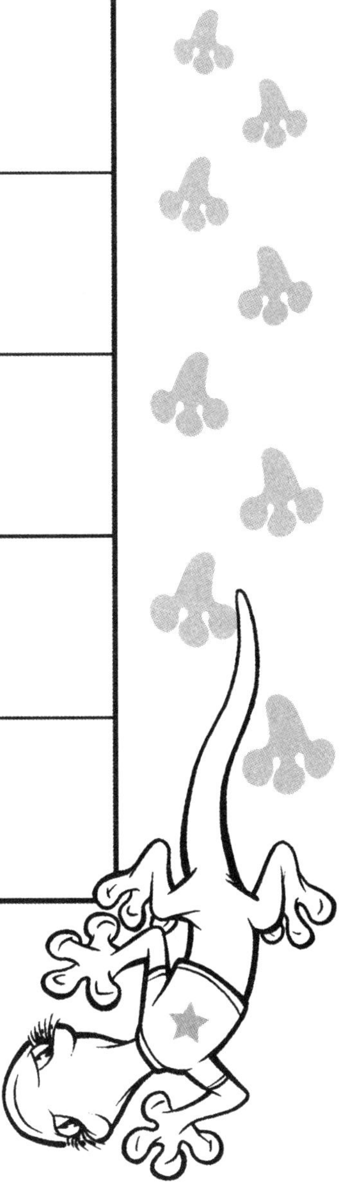

Use what you have learned to determine how many squares there would be on a checkerboard (an eight by eight grid).

# The Square Challenge

*Answer the following questions about the grid on the first page. Use the back of the paper if necessary.*

1. How many different sizes of squares are there in the grid? List them below.

2. How many squares of each size are there? Make a list.

3. What patterns do you see in these numbers? Describe some of these patterns.

4. How many squares are there total in the grid?

5. Describe the method you used to determine this answer.

6. Use what you have learned to determine the number of squares of all sizes there are on a checkerboard. Show your work.

# The Square Challenge

Cut out the squares below. Use them to help you determine the total number of squares in the grid on the first page.

JUST FOR THE FUN OF IT! BOOK TWO  39  © 2010 AIMS Education Foundation

# The Square Challenge

## Connecting Learning

1. How many different sizes of squares are there in the grid?

2. How many squares of each size are there in the grid?

3. What patterns do you see in these numbers?

4. How many squares of all sizes are there in the grid?

5. What methods did you use to count the squares?

6. How do you know that you counted all of the squares?

7. How many squares of all sizes are there in a checkerboard?

8. How did you determine this value?

# Lines, Triangles, and Squares, Oh My!

**Topic**
Geometry

**Key Question**
Into how many regions can a square be divided by a given number of straight lines?

**Learning Goals**
Students will:
- find all of the regions into which a square can be divided with any number of straight lines,
- discover some geometric principles, and
- be challenged to find algebraic explanations for their work.

**Guiding Document**
NCTM Standards 2000*
- *Investigate, describe, and reason about the results of subdividing, combining, and transforming shapes*
- *Build new mathematical knowledge through problem solving*
- *Apply and adapt a variety of appropriate strategies to solve problems*

**Math**
Geometry and spatial sense
Problem solving

**Integrated Processes**
Observing
Collecting and recording data
Interpreting data
Generalizing

**Problem-Solving Strategies**
Use manipulatives
Look for patterns
Organize the information
　make a table
Work backwards
Wish for an easier problem

**Materials**
Rulers
Flat toothpicks or paper strips (see *Management 1*)
Student pages

**Background Information**
This activity is a modification of a standard problem from geometry. A typical high school geometry text might state the problem as follows: *Into how many regions do "n" lines, no two of which are parallel, and no three of which intersect in the same point, divide the plane?* This problem is a great one, and challenges most geometry students. (It's quite easy to see that one line divides a plane into two regions and that two lines divide a plane into four regions, but it's harder to visualize three lines dividing a plane into seven regions and four lines dividing it into 11!)

To make this problem accessible to younger students, it has been modified by limiting the problem to a plane figure—the square—instead of the entire plane, and by taking away the prohibition against parallel lines and no three lines intersecting at the same point. This modification not only makes the problem appropriate for middle school and upper elementary students, it also makes it more open-ended. Amazingly, this *easier* version turns out to be a *richer* problem than the original one.

**Management**
1. To assist your students in finding all the possible regions for a given number of lines, they will need either thin strips of paper (≈ 6.5 cm x 0.2 cm) or flat toothpicks. These can be arranged on top of the square provided on the second student page to discover many different solutions without continuously drawing and erasing lines. Paper strips may work better than toothpicks because they continue to lay flat even when crossed over each other. If the paper strips are a color other than white, they will be easier to see.
2. Students will need rulers or straight edges to record their solutions neatly and accurately.
3. This activity can be done using either an open-ended or a more structured approach. For an open-ended approach, give students only the first two student pages. These pages simply introduce the problem and provide spaces in which to record solutions. For a more structured approach, use all of the pages. The additional page should provide enough structure to help students as they work on this problem.

JUST FOR THE FUN OF IT! BOOK TWO

## Procedure

1. Distribute the student pages and make sure everyone understands the instructions. *Into how many different numbers of regions can three lines divide a square? How about four lines? How about five or more lines?*
2. Hand out at least six paper strips or toothpicks to each student and give them sufficient time to work on the problem.
3. Close with a time of class discussion where students share their solutions and their discoveries. If some possibilities for the number of regions have been overlooked for lower numbers of lines (four and five), guide the class into group discovery of them (see *Solutions*).

## Connecting Learning

1. How many different numbers of regions are possible for four lines? [7] What are they? [5-11]
2. How many different numbers of regions are possible for five lines? …six lines? What are they? (See *Solutions*.)
3. What did you do to get the fewest regions for each number of lines? [Put the lines parallel, or so they don't intersect.]
4. What did you do to get the most regions for each number of lines? [Have the lines intersect as many times as possible.]

## Extensions

1. Examine the shapes of the regions formed by the lines (triangle, quadrilateral, pentagon, hexagon, etc.) and see if there is a pattern to these shapes. (See *Solutions*.)
2. Find the maximum and minimum number of intersections for any given number of lines and relate these numbers to the number of regions. (See *Solutions*.)
3. Have older students find the algebraic formulas for determining the minimum and maximum number of regions for *n* lines. (See *Solutions*.)
4. Challenge advanced students to determine the algebraic generalization that relates the number of lines to the total number of solutions possible. (See *Solutions*.)

## Solutions

The diagrams below represent all of the possible numbers of regions for four and five lines. Keep in mind that the lines may be arranged any number of ways and still yield the same number of regions. These diagrams are not the "right" answers, but some of the many possible correct solutions.

### Four Lines

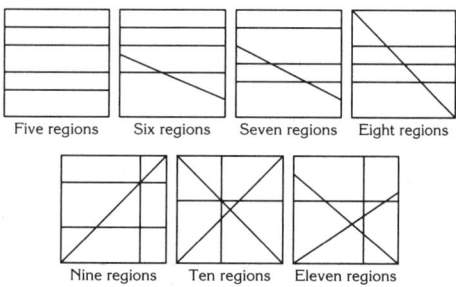

### Five Lines

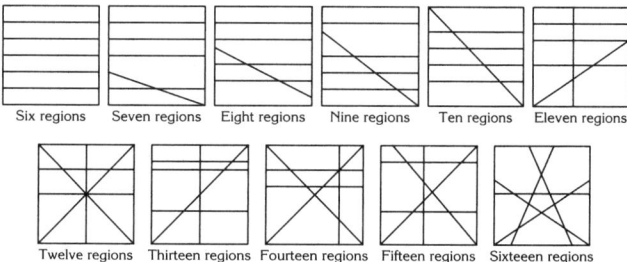

### Student page three

| # of Lines | Regions Possible |
|---|---|
| 0 | 1 |
| 1 | 2 |
| 2 | 3, 4 |
| 3 | 4, 5, 6, 7 |
| 4 | 5-11 |
| 5 | 6-16 |
| 6 | 7-22 |

| # of Lines Used | Total # of Solutions Possible |
|---|---|
| 0 | 1 |
| 1 | 1 |
| 2 | 2 |
| 3 | 4 |
| 4 | 7 |
| 5 | 11 |
| 6 | 16 |

Following are some observations about the nature of the problem, as well as solutions to some of the extensions.

1. To achieve the minimum number of regions, the lines must be parallel or not intersect within the square.
2. To achieve the maximum number of regions, each line must cross as many other lines as possible at a different point.
3. The formula for determining the minimum number of regions for $n$ lines is $n + 1$. For determining the maximum number of regions, the formula is $[n(n + 1)/2] + 1$.
4. The minimum number of intersections for any number of lines is always zero. The maximum number of intersections is $n(n - 1)/2$, which is related to the formula for the triangular numbers.

| # of Lines | Minimum # of intersections | Maximum # of intersections |
|---|---|---|
| 1 | 0 | 0 |
| 2 | 0 | 1 |
| 3 | 0 | 3 |
| 4 | 0 | 6 |
| 5 | 0 | 10 |
| 6 | 0 | 15 |
| $n$ | 0 | $n(n-1)/2$ |

5. The formula that relates the number of lines used to the total number of solutions possible is $[n(n + 1)/2)] - [n + (n + 1)] + n$.

*Solutions for Extension #1*
When looking at the different possibilities for shapes of regions made from different numbers of lines there are virtually infinite solutions. Almost every new way you arrange the lines gives a different answer. Because of this, only solutions for two lines are explored here. Again, the actual placement of the lines may vary, but the types of shapes created are the same. What you begin to discover is that there are different patterns for the regions created by intersecting and non-intersecting lines. There is also a maximum and minimum sum (reached by adding the numbers of the sides together) achievable for a given number of lines. (For the purposes of discussion, lines that meet at the edge of the square are considered to be non-intersecting.)

For each diagram: Triangle = 3, Quadrilateral = 4, Pentagon = 5, Hexagon = 6

**Non-intersecting possibilities**

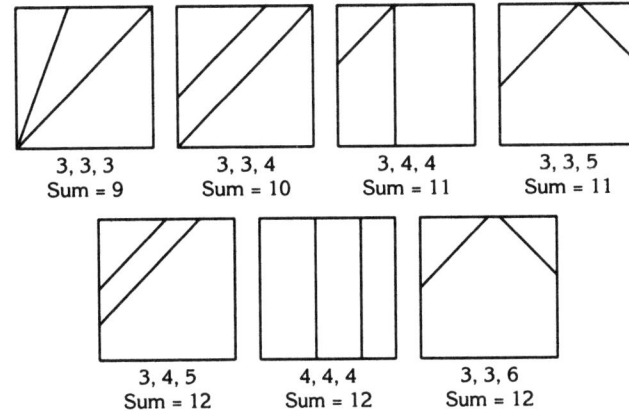

**Intersecting possibilities**

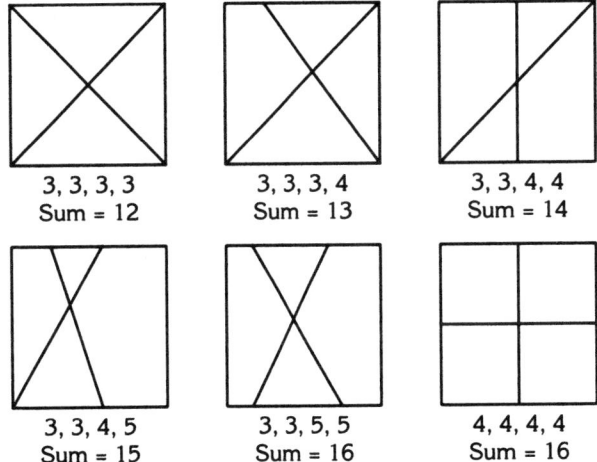

\* Reprinted with permission from *Principles and Standards for School Mathematics*, 2000 by the National Council of Teachers of Mathematics. All rights reserved.

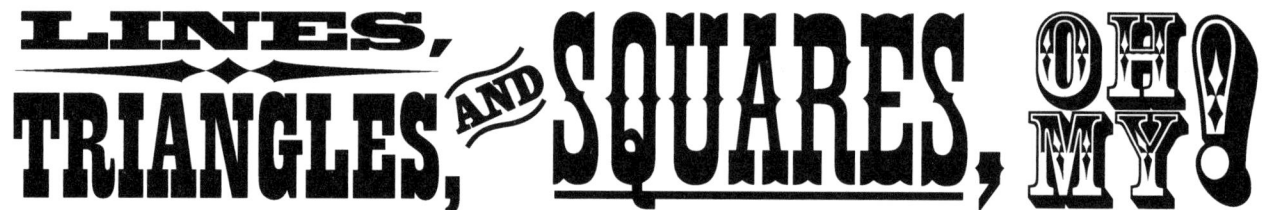

# Lines, Triangles, and Squares, Oh My!

## Key Question

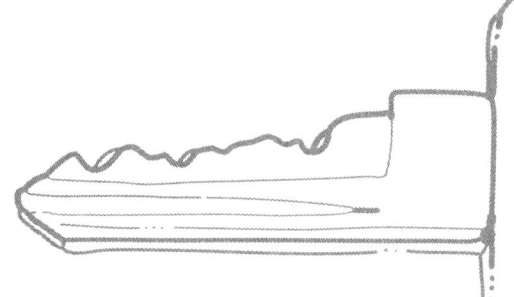

Into how many regions can a square be divided by a given number of straight lines?

## Learning Goals

### Students will:

- find all of the regions into which a square can be divided with any number of straight lines,

- discover some geometric principles, and

- be challenged to find algebraic explanations for their work.

# LINES, TRIANGLES, AND SQUARES, OH MY!

One straight line can only divide a square into two regions. Two straight lines, however, can divide a square into either three or four regions, as shown below. Into how many different numbers of regions can three lines divide a square? How about four lines? How about five or more lines? What do you discover when answering these questions?

**Challenge:** Explore this problem in as great a depth as possible. Be prepared to share your findings with others.

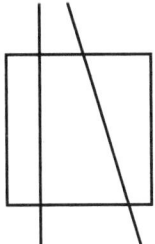
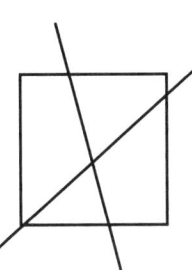

# LINES, TRIANGLES, AND SQUARES, OH MY!

Use thin strips of paper or flat toothpicks on the larger square below to find your solutions for any given number of lines. Use your ruler to make a record of your solutions in the smaller squares below.

_____  _____  _____  _____  _____
# of lines   # of lines   # of lines   # of lines   # of lines
_____  _____  _____  _____  _____
# of regions # of regions # of regions # of regions # of regions

_____  _____  _____  _____  _____
# of lines   # of lines   # of lines   # of lines   # of lines
_____  _____  _____  _____  _____
# of regions # of regions # of regions # of regions # of regions

_____  _____  _____  _____  _____
# of lines   # of lines   # of lines   # of lines   # of lines
_____  _____  _____  _____  _____
# of regions # of regions # of regions # of regions # of regions

JUST FOR THE FUN OF IT! BOOK TWO            46            © 2010 AIMS Education Foundation

Use the following tables to help you organize your findings.

| # of Lines | Regions Possible |
|---|---|
| 0 | 1 |
| 1 | 2 |
| 2 | 3, 4 |
| 3 | |
| 4 | |
| 5 | |
| 6 | |

| # of Lines Used | Total # of Solutions Possible |
|---|---|
| 0 | 1 |
| 1 | 1 |
| 2 | 2 |
| 3 | |
| 4 | |
| 5 | |
| 6 | |

Think of some other questions that are related to this problem. Pick one of these questions to explore and report your findings to others in the class.

## Connecting Learning

1. How many different numbers of regions are possible for four lines? What are they?

2. How many different numbers of regions are possible for five lines? …six lines? What are they?

3. What did you do to get the fewest regions for each number of lines?

4. What did you do to get the most regions for each number of lines?

# Set Counting

**Topics**
Counting, sets

**Key Questions**
1. What are all the possible ways 14 objects can be placed into two separate sets (groups)?
2. What are all the possible ways 14 objects can be placed into three separate sets (groups)?

**Learning Goals**
Students will:
- find all the possible ways to put 14 objects into two and three sets, and
- discover the benefits of a systematic approach to problem solving as opposed to trial-and-error methods.

**Guiding Document**
*NCTM Standards 2000\**
- *Build new mathematical knowledge through problem solving*
- *Apply and adapt a variety of appropriate strategies to solve problems*

**Math**
Counting
Sets
Number sentences, optional

**Integrated Processes**
Observing
Classifying
Collecting and recording data
Generalizing

**Problem-Solving Strategies**
Organize the information
Use manipulatives

**Materials**
Small objects such as beans, 14 per student
Student pages
Overhead transparency, optional

**Background Information**
To mathematicians, a set is simply a collection of objects. Two or more sets can be discrete (non-overlapping), intersecting (overlapping), or one set can be a subset (completely contained within) of another. In this activity, students will be placing 14 objects into two, and then three, discrete (non-overlapping) sets. While this set knowledge is not the main focus of the activity, older students could be challenged to see how a set of eight objects that intersects (overlaps) a second set of 10 objects can have a total of 14 objects between them (if the intersection of these sets has four objects).

The main focus of this activity is to help students develop a systematic way to solve the problem(s) at hand. Trial and error can be used in the first part, since it is easy to distribute the 14 objects between two sets. However, using this same approach for three sets will probably not work. (There are 24 solutions for the second part and it is not likely that students will find all of these solutions without coming up with some organized way to approach the problem.)

For the purposes of this activity, order does not make a difference. For example, placing nine objects in the top set and five in the bottom would be considered the same distribution as placing five objects in the top set and nine in the bottom.

**Management**
1. Students can use any small objects to place in the sets (shapes) on the student pages. If you are doing this activity near a holiday you can make it seasonal by using festive candies such as Valentine hearts or Christmas chocolates.
2. To introduce the activity, you may want to display the student pages using a projection device and go over a few examples as a class.
3. When introducing this activity, make sure students understand that the order in which objects are placed into the sets does not make a difference. (See *Background Information*.)
4. This activity is divided into two parts in an attempt to increase students' awareness of the benefits of systematic problem solving. In the first part, it is easy for students to come up with all of the possible ways to distribute the 14 objects between two sets using trial and error. However, in the second part, it is much more difficult to find all of the ways to put the 14 objects into three sets using trial and error. Because of this, it is important to discuss the benefits of a organizing the information before the students begin *Part Two*.

## Procedure

*Part One*
1. Distribute the first student page and make sure students understand the instructions. *Place the 14 objects given to you into the two sets in as many different ways as you can. Make a record of each different way. Remember that in this activity, order doesn't make a difference.*
2. If necessary, find a few of the ways as a class.
3. Give students sufficient time to find all of the possible ways for two groups, making sure that they are keeping an accurate record of their work. They can record their answers as pairs (e.g., 5, 9; 1, 13; 11, 3).
4. Have students share their answers and the methods they used.
5. Hand out the second student page and use it and the discussion questions for *Part One* to help students see the value of an organized approach.

*Part Two*
1. Distribute the third student page and challenge students to find all the possible ways 14 objects can be placed into three sets using the systematic approach they developed on the second student page or some other similar method.
2. Have students share their solutions for placing 14 objects into three sets. If any are missing (see *Solutions*), help students discover them. Close with a final time of group discussion and sharing.

## Connecting Learning

*Part One*
1. How many ways did you discover to place 14 objects into two sets? [Eight ways are possible if order doesn't make a difference.]
2. How do you know that you found them all? [Various. Used every number, developed a system, etc.]
3. How did you go about finding the various solutions? [Various. Trial and error, systematic, etc.]
4. For those who used a system, how did you decide upon your method?
5. How did your system help you to solve the problem more easily? [Various. Helped us see what had already been used, etc.]

*Part Two*
1. How many solutions did you discover for three sets? [Twenty-four are possible.]
2. How did using a systematic approach help you solve the problem?
3. What are the benefits of organizing information over trial and error? [Various. Gives you a way to be sure you have found all of the solutions, you don't waste time by repeating answers, etc.]

## Extensions

1. For younger students, use a number smaller than 14 for *Part Two*.
2. Write each of the solutions as a number sentence. For example, 9 + 5 = 14, 8 + 6 = 14, etc.
3. Have older students find all of the combinations of 14 objects divided into four sets.
4. Challenge older students to find all of the permutations of triplets that add to 14. This is quite a difficult task since there are either three (for triplets with a repeated number like 6, 4, 4) or six (for all other triplets) permutations for each combination.

## Solutions

*Part One*
For 14 objects and two sets, the possible solutions** are:
1. **14, 0** (0, 14)
2. **13, 1** (1, 13)
3. **12, 2** (2, 12)
4. **11, 3** (3, 11)
5. **10, 4** (4, 10)
6. **9, 5** (5, 9)
7. **8, 6** (6, 8)
8. **7, 7**

*Part Two*
For 14 objects and three sets, the possible solutions** are:
1. **14, 0, 0** (0, 14, 0) (0, 0, 14)
2. **13, 1, 0** (13, 0, 1) (1, 13, 0) (1, 0, 13) (0, 1, 13) (0, 13, 1)
3. **12, 2, 0** (12, 0, 2) (0, 12, 2) (0, 2, 12) (2, 0, 12) (2, 12, 0)
4. **12, 1, 1** (1, 12, 1) (1, 1, 12)
5. **11, 3, 0** (11, 0, 3) (3, 11, 0) (3, 0, 11) (0, 11, 3) (0, 3, 11)
6. **11, 2, 1** (11, 1, 2) (1, 2, 11) (1, 11, 2) (2, 1, 11) (2, 11, 1)
7. **10, 4, 0** (10, 0, 4) (0, 4, 10) (0, 10, 4) (4, 0, 10) (4, 10, 0)
8. **10, 3, 1** (10, 1, 3) (3, 10, 1) (3, 1, 10) (1, 10, 3) (1, 3, 10)
9. **10, 2, 2** (2, 10, 2) (2, 2, 10)
10. **9, 5, 0** (9, 0, 5) (0, 9, 5) (0, 5, 9) (5, 0, 9) (5, 9, 0)
11. **9, 4, 1** (9, 1, 4) (1, 4, 9) (1, 9, 4) (4, 1, 9) (4, 9, 1)
12. **9, 3, 2** (9, 2, 3) (2, 3, 9) (2, 9, 3) (3, 2, 9) (3, 9, 2)
13. **8, 6, 0** (8, 0, 6) (0, 8, 6) (0, 6, 8) (6, 0, 8) (6, 8, 0)
14. **8, 5, 1** (8, 1, 5) (1, 5, 8) (1, 8, 5) (5, 1, 8) (5, 8, 1)
15. **8, 4, 2** (8, 2, 4) (2, 4, 8) (2, 8, 4) (4, 8, 2) (4, 2, 8)
16. **8, 3, 3** (3, 8, 3) (3, 3, 8)
17. **7, 7, 0** (7, 0, 7) (0, 7, 7)
18. **7, 6, 1** (7, 1, 6) (1, 7, 6) (1, 6, 7) (6, 7, 1) (6, 1, 7)
19. **7, 5, 2** (7, 2, 5) (2, 5, 7) (2, 7, 5) (5, 2, 7) (5, 7, 2)
20. **7, 4, 3** (7, 3, 4) (3, 4, 7) (3, 7, 4) (4, 3, 7) (4, 7, 3)
21. **6, 6, 2** (2, 6, 6) (6, 2, 6)
22. **6, 5, 3** (6, 3, 5) (3, 5, 6) (3, 6, 5) (5, 3, 6) (5, 6, 3)
23. **6, 4, 4** (4, 6, 4) (4, 4, 6)
24. **5, 5, 4** (5, 4, 5) (4, 5, 5)

\* Reprinted with permission from *Principles and Standards for School Mathematics*, 2000 by the National Council of Teachers of Mathematics. All rights reserved.

\*\* Since order doesn't make a difference in this activity, any of the solutions in a given line above is correct. However, only one solution (per line) can be counted toward the total. The bold numbers simply indicate one system used to come up with the different solutions.

# SET COUNTING

## Key Questions

1. What are all the possible ways 14 objects can be placed into two separate sets (groups)?
2. What are all the possible ways 14 objects can be placed into three separate sets (groups)?

## Learning Goals

### Students will:

- find all the possible ways to put 14 objects into two and three sets, and

- discover the benefits of a systematic approach to problem solving as opposed to trial-and-error methods.

# SET COUNTING

## Warm-Up:
Place 14 objects in different ways into the two sets shown here. Make a record of each solution. Note: Order doesn't matter in this activity.

## My Solutions:

Have you found all of the possible ways to arrange the objects?

How do you know?

# SET COUNTING

In problem solving, a systematic (organized) approach often works better than using trial and error. Think about the problem you have just done. How could you do this problem in a more organized or systematic way? Describe this below.

Share your method with others in the class.

Now, use your method to do the harder problem on the next page.

JUST FOR THE FUN OF IT! BOOK TWO          53          © 2010 AIMS Education Foundation

# SET COUNTING

## Main Challenge
Place your 14 objects in various ways into the three spaces below. Make a record of each solution.

## My Solutions:

# SET  COUNTING

## Connecting Learning

*Part One*

1. How many ways did you discover to place 14 objects into two sets?

2. How do you know that you found them all?

3. How did you go about finding the various solutions?

4. For those who used a system, how did you decide upon your method?

5. How did your system help you to solve the problem more easily?

# SET COUNTING

## Connecting Learning

*Part Two*

1. How many solutions did you discover for three sets?

2. How did using a systematic approach help you solve the problem?

3. What are the benefits of organizing information over trial and error?

# Calendar Counts

**Topic**
Patterns

**Key Question**
How many ones are there in the month of January when the dates are written in abbreviated form? (For example, 1/15/10.)

**Learning Goals**
Students will:
- be challenged to count the number of ones in the month of January when the dates are written in abbreviated form,
- explore number patterns, and
- practice their basic computational skills.

**Guiding Documents**
*Project 2061 Benchmarks*
- *Mathematics is the study of many kinds of patterns, including numbers and shapes and operations on them. Sometimes patterns are studied because they help to explain how the world works or how to solve practical problems, sometimes because they are interesting in themselves.*
- *Add, subtract, multiply, and divide whole numbers mentally and on paper.*

*NCTM Standards 2000\**
- *Describe, extend, and make generalizations about geometric and numeric patterns*
- *Build new mathematical knowledge through problem solving*
- *Solve problems that arise in mathematics and in other contexts*
- *Apply and adapt a variety of appropriate strategies to solve problems*

**Math**
Counting
Math patterns
Problem solving

**Integrated Processes**
Observing
Collecting and recording data
Generalizing

**Problem-Solving Strategies**
Organize the information
Look for patterns

**Materials**
Calendars, one per group
Student pages

**Background Information**
*Calendar Counts* has students explore numerical patterns in calendar dates. As they do this, they also explore the American system of abbreviating dates using three numbers separated by dashes or back slashes. In our system, the month, numbered from one to 12, comes first. This is followed by the day of the month. The year is written next with only the last two digits showing. Many other countries use a slightly different system with the day of the month first, followed by the month, and then the year.

After students count the ones in the month of January, they will be challenged to generalize their techniques to help them count the number of ones in a calendar year. They will also use these techniques to answer questions that they raise themselves about calendar number patterns.

**Management**
1. Each group should have access to a calendar. Although a calendar is not absolutely necessary, it will make the task easier for students.
2. To help students remember the number of days in each month without looking at a calendar the following rhyme may help: "Thirty days hath September, April, June, and November. All the rest have 31, save for February with 28 days clear, and 29 each each leap year."
3. The second student page is completely open-ended, and challenges students to think of their own questions to explore. Some suggestions are provided in the *Extensions* section.

**Procedure**
1. Distribute the first student page and go over the instructions. *How many ones are there in the month of January when the dates are written in abbreviated form?*
2. Have students get into small groups and hand out the calendars. Give the groups sufficient time to complete both parts of the first page.
3. Hand out the second student page (if desired) and have students think of extensions for their groups to explore.

JUST FOR THE FUN OF IT! BOOK TWO © 2010 AIMS Education Foundation

4. When all groups have had time to explore at least one extension, close with a time of class discussion where students share their findings and the method(s) that they used to arrive at their solutions.

**Connecting Learning**
1. How many ones are there in the month of January? [45 for years that do not have a one in the last two digits, 76 for years with a one in the last two digits, 107 for years ending in 11.]
2. How did you come up with this number?
3. How many ones are there in this year? [316 for years without a one in the last two digits, 681 for years with a one in the last two digits, 1046 for years ending in 11.]
4. How did you come up with this number?
5. What patterns did you see in this problem? (See *Solutions*.)
6. How did these patterns help you count the number of ones?

**Extensions**
These extensions are some that students can explore during the second part of this activity. Hopefully the questions students explore will be generated by the students themselves, but if not, the following suggestions can be used.
1. Are there the same number of ones each year?
2. How many ones are there in this decade?
3. How many ones are there in the twentieth century? The twenty-first century?
4. How many ones were there in 1991? How many ones will there be in 2111?
5. How many twos are there in this year?

**Solutions**
These solutions are written for a year that does not have a one in the last two digits. The solutions for years such as 1991 or 2001 would be different.

*Part One*
There are 45 ones in the month of January when the year does not have a one in the last two digits.

1/1  1/2  1/3  1/4  1/5  1/6  1/7  1/8
1/9  1/10  1/11  1/12  1/13  1/14  1/15  1/16
1/17  1/18  1/19  1/20  1/21  1/22  1/23  1/24
1/25  1/26  1/27  1/28  1/29  1/30  1/31

- 31 of these ones are from the month, 14 are from the day. Of the 14 that are from the day, 10 are in the tens place, and four are in the ones place.
- Years that have a one in the last two digits (2001, 2010, 2021, etc.) have 76 ones in the months of January.
- Years that have two ones in the last two digits (2011) have 107 ones in the month of January.

*Part Two*
There are 316 ones in each year that does not have a one in the last two digits. There are 681 ones in each year that has a one in the last two digits (682 in leap years). There are 1046 ones in each year that has two ones in the last two digits.

There are eight months that do not have a one in the month (February to September). Of those eight months, those that have 30 or fewer days (February, April, June, September) each have 13 ones.

1  2  3  4  5  6  7  8  9  10  11  12
13  14  15  16  17  18  19  20  21  22  23  24
25  26  27  28  29  30

Those months that have 31 days (March, May, July, August) each have 14 ones.

1  2  3  4  5  6  7  8  9  10  11  12
13  14  15  16  17  18  19  20  21  22  23  24
25  26  27  28  29  30  31

Those months that have a one in the month (January, October and December) each have 45 ones. November has 73 ones because of the double one in the month.

11/1  11/2  11/3  11/4  11/5  11/6  11/7
11/8  11/9  11/10  11/11  11/12  11/13  11/14
11/15  11/16  11/17  11/18  11/19  11/2  11/21
11/22  11/23  11/24  11/25  11/26  11/27  11/28
11/29  11/30

| Years with no ones in the last digits | |
|---|---|
| Month | # of ones |
| January | 45 |
| February | 13 |
| March | 14 |
| April | 13 |
| May | 14 |
| June | 13 |
| July | 14 |
| August | 14 |
| September | 13 |
| October | 45 |
| November | 73 |
| December | 45 |
| Total | 316 |

| Years with one one in the last digits | |
|---|---|
| Month | # of ones |
| January | 76 |
| February | 41 (42) |
| March | 45 |
| April | 43 |
| May | 45 |
| June | 43 |
| July | 45 |
| August | 45 |
| September | 43 |
| October | 76 |
| November | 103 |
| December | 76 |
| Total | 681 (682) |

| Years with two ones in the last digits | |
|---|---|
| Month | # of ones |
| January | 107 |
| February | 69 (71) |
| March | 76 |
| April | 73 |
| May | 76 |
| June | 73 |
| July | 76 |
| August | 76 |
| September | 73 |
| October | 107 |
| November | 133 |
| December | 107 |
| Total | 1046 (1048) |

Numbers in (parentheses) are for leap years.

* Reprinted with permission from *Principles and Standards for School Mathematics*, 2000 by the National Council of Teachers of Mathematics. All rights reserved.

# Calendar Counts

## Key Question

How many ones are there in the month of January when the dates are written in abbreviated form? (For example, 1/15/10.)

## Learning Goals

### Students will:

- be challenged to count the number of ones in the month of January when the dates are written in abbreviated form,

- explore number patterns, and

- practice their basic computational skills.

# Calendar Counts

Dates are often written using several numbers separated by slashes. For example, Martin Luther King Junior's birth date—January 15, 1929—can be written as 1/15/29. Using this method of writing the date, how many ones are there in the month of January this year? Show your work below.

How many ones are there in the entire year when using this method of writing the date? Show your work on the back of this page.

# Calendar Counts

Think of your own calendar question to explore. Write it down and use the space below to record your findings.

Question:

Findings:

## Connecting Learning

1. How many ones are there in the month of January?

2. How did you come up with this number?

3. How many ones are there in this year?

4. How did you come up with this number?

5. What patterns did you see in this problem?

6. How did these patterns help you count the number of ones?

# Tinkering with Twos

**Topic**
Problem solving

**Key Question**
How can you combine five twos with one or more basic arithmetic symbols so that the resulting number sentences produce the numbers one to 10?

**Learning Goal**
Students will be challenged to use five twos together with various mathematical operations to make number sentences resulting in the numbers one through 10.

**Guiding Documents**
*Project 2061 Benchmarks*
- *Add, subtract, multiply, and divide whole numbers mentally, on paper, and with a calculator.*
- *The operations + and – are inverses of each other— one undoes what the other does; likewise x and ÷.*

*NCTM Standards 2000\**
- *Identify and use relationships between operations, such as division as the inverse of multiplication, to solve problems*
- *Understand and use the inverse relationships of addition and subtraction, multiplication and division, and squaring and finding square roots to simplify computations and solve problems*
- *Build new mathematical knowledge through problem solving*

**Math**
Whole number operations
    addition
    subtraction
    multiplication
    division
Number sense
Order of operations
Problem solving

**Integrated Processes**
Observing
Recording
Relating
Generalizing

**Problem Solving Strategies**
Write a number sentence
Guess and check

**Materials**
Student pages

**Background Information**
This activity allows students to practice mathematical skills in a problem-solving setting as they are challenged to put five twos together with mathematical symbols to make number sentences, each producing a number from one to 10. The twos can be grouped together (e.g., 22 or 222) or used separately, but each number sentence should use exactly five. The symbols used need not be limited to the basic operations and might include things such as radicals, powers, and factorials. In addition to helping students practice basic computation and problem-solving skills, this activity is a good exercise in order of operations. The extensions your students think of can take the original problem in many different directions and produce a rich mathematical environment in your classroom.

**Management**
1. The abilities of your students are the only boundary on this problem. The operations used by students can be as simple as the basic four arithmetic operations, or as advanced as powers and square roots. Challenge your students to try new things as they create their number sentences.
2. Students will need to use parentheses and brackets to create the correct order of operations. If your students are not familiar with how orders of operations work, be sure to go over the concept before beginning.
3. For the more advanced students who may wish to use powers, they should know that the power can be a number other than two. If they do raise something to the second power, the power does not count as one of their five twos.

**Procedure**
1. Hand out the student pages and go over the instructions. *Combine five twos with one or more arithmetic symbol(s) to make number sentences that produce each of the numbers from one to 10. You may use brackets and parentheses if necessary. You may also group numbers together (22, 222, etc.).*

JUST FOR THE FUN OF IT! BOOK TWO     63     © 2010 AIMS Education Foundation

2. Have students work together in groups to create their number sentences. When one group member discovers a solution, each person in the group should record it on his or her paper. Encourage students to get as many different number sentences as possible for each number.
3. When all groups have found at least one solution for all of the numbers from one to 10 and have had time to describe their processes, have a time of class discussion and sharing.
4. After students have given several suggestions for extensions, pick one to explore as a class, or allow individual groups to choose their own to explore.

### Connecting Learning
1. What number sentences were you able to come up with that had as their result the numbers one to 10? (See *Solutions*.)
2. Describe the process you used to approach this problem.
3. Which number(s) was (were) the hardest for you to find number sentences for? Why do you think this is?
4. Which number(s) was (were) the easiest for you to find number sentences for? Why do you think this is?
5. What extensions can you think of for this activity?

### Extensions
Ideally these extensions will come from your students, but if they are having trouble thinking of some, the following are a few suggestions.
1. Use four or six twos instead of five.
2. Use a number other than two in the number sentences.
3. Make the numbers 11 to 20.
4. For older students, try to use a power, square root, etc., in every solution.

### Solutions
There are almost endless possibilities for number sentences using five twos and resulting in the numbers from one to 10. Two examples are given for each number, one that uses only the four basic operations, and one that uses more advanced operations.

**One**
$2(2 \div 2) - (2 \div 2)$ $\qquad \dfrac{(22 - 2^4)}{(2^2 + 2)}$

**Two**
$\dfrac{(2 + 2 + 2) - 2}{2}$ $\qquad 22 - (2^4 + 2) - 2$

**Three**
$2 - 2 + 2 + (2 \div 2)$ $\qquad \dfrac{22 - (2^2 \times 2^2)}{2}$

**Four**
$\dfrac{(2 \times 2) + 2 + 2}{2}$ $\qquad \dfrac{(2^2 + 2^2 + 2^2) - 2^2}{2}$

**Five**
$2 + 2 + 2 - (2 \div 2)$ $\qquad \dfrac{2^4 - (2 + 2 + 2)}{2}$

**Six**
$\dfrac{2(2 + 2 + 2)}{2}$ $\qquad 2^4 - 2^3 - 2^2 + 2^0 + 2^0$

**Seven**
$(2 \times 2 \times 2) - (2 \div 2)$ $\qquad \dfrac{22 - (2^2 \times 2)}{2}$

**Eight**
$\dfrac{(2 + 2)(2 + 2)}{2}$ $\qquad \dfrac{\sqrt{2^4} \times (2 + 2^0 + 2^0)}{2}$

**Nine**
$(2 \times 2 \times 2) + (2 \div 2)$ $\qquad \dfrac{2(2^2 + 2^2) + 2}{2}$

**Ten**
$2 + 2 + 2 + 2 + 2$ $\qquad \dfrac{22 - 2}{2^0 + 2^0}$

\* Reprinted with permission from *Principles and Standards for School Mathematics*, 2000 by the National Council of Teachers of Mathematics. All rights reserved.

### Key Question

How can you combine five twos with one or more basic arithmetic symbols so that the resulting number sentences produce the numbers one to 10?

## Learning Goal

### Students will:

be challenged to use five twos together with various mathematical operations to make number sentences resulting in the numbers one through 10.

# Tinkering with Twos

Combine five twos with one or more arithmetic symbol(s) (+, −, ×, ÷, etc.) so that the resulting number sentences produce the numbers one through 10. For example, (2 ÷ 2) + (2 ÷ 2) ÷ 2 = 1. See if you can find a different way to get one. (There are several ways to get each number.) Next, try to find solutions for each of the numbers from two to 10. Use the space below to record your solutions.

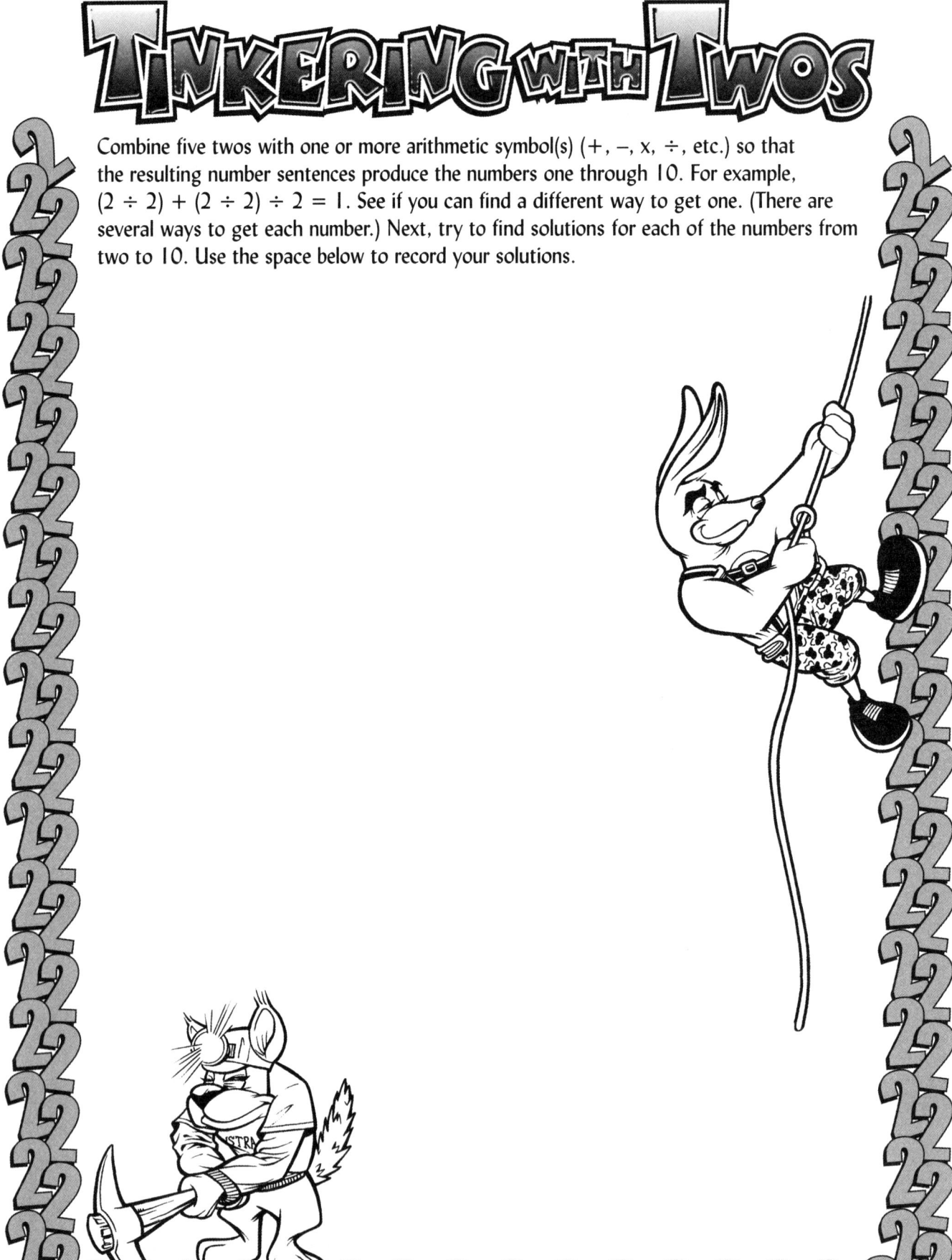

1. Describe the processes and techniques you used to solve this problem.

2. List some extensions that you can think of for this activity.

3. Select one extension and explore it. Report your results below.

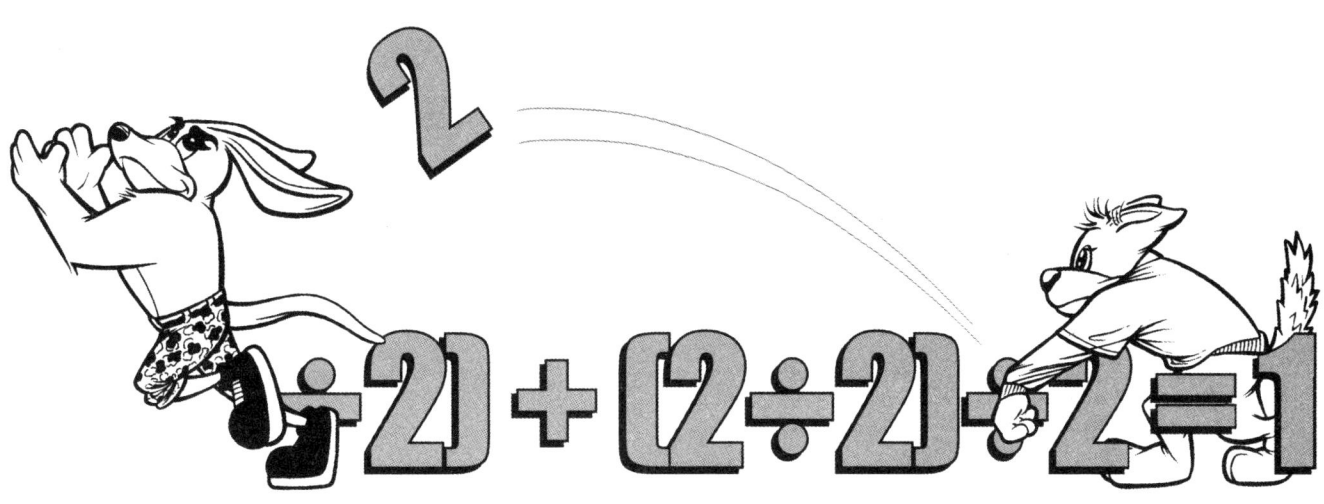

## Connecting Learning

1. What number sentences were you able to come up with that had as their result the numbers one to 10?

2. Describe the process you used to approach this problem.

3. Which number(s) was (were) the hardest for you to find number sentences for? Why do you think this is?

4. Which number(s) was (were) the easiest for you to find number sentences for? Why do you think this is?

5. What extensions can you think of for this activity?

# Making a Difference 2

## Topic
Problem solving

## Key Question
How can you arrange the numbers from one to six in a triangular array so that the difference of any two adjacent numbers appears below those two numbers?

## Learning Goals
Students will:
- discover how to arrange the numbers from one to six in a triangular array so that each succeeding row is generated by the difference between neighboring numbers from the row above it, and
- be challenged to do the same thing using the numbers one to 10.

## Guiding Documents
*Project 2061 Benchmark*
- *Usually there is no one right way to solve a mathematical problem; different methods have different advantages and disadvantages.*

*NCTM Standards 2000\**
- *Apply and adapt a variety of appropriate strategies to solve problems*
- *Build new mathematical knowledge through problem solving*

## Math
Whole number operations
Differences
Odd and even
Problem solving

## Integrated Processes
Observing
Comparing and contrasting
Inferring
Relating
Generalizing

## Problem-Solving Strategies
Use manipulatives
Guess and check
Look for patterns
Use logical thinking

## Materials
Number cards, one to 10
Student pages

## Background Information
In this activity, students must place the numbers from one to six in a triangular array so that the number below any two adjacent numbers is the difference between them. The solutions for the numbers one to six are fairly simple, and may be reached by basic trial and error. However, students are additionally challenged to try and solve the problem using the numbers from one to 10—a much more difficult problem that will necessitate the development of a systematic approach in order to be solved.

Older students can also be challenged to think about the problem in a more abstract way as they look at the odd and even numbers and how they must be arranged. This can lead to informal proofs and algebraic thinking.

## Management
1. Students will each need number cards from one to 10 for this activity. The cards can be made from scratch paper cut into rectangles of the appropriate size to fit into the spaces on the student pages.
2. Be sure to assess the ability of your class before you determine how in-depth to study this problem. There are many powerful extensions dealing with the nature of odd and even numbers, but these may not be appropriate for younger students. Younger students may also have a difficult time finding a solution for the second part of the activity, which uses the numbers one to 10.

## Procedure
1. Have students make their number cards from one to 10, and hand out the first student page and the solutions page. Go over the instructions and be sure that everyone understands the rules of the activity.
2. Have students work together in small groups to discover as many different solutions as possible for the numbers one to six. Encourage them to pay careful attention to the arrangement of the numbers so that they do not record duplicate solutions.

3. When groups have all discovered at least two of the solutions for six numbers, hand out the second student page and have groups work on finding solutions using the numbers one to 10. Be sure to allow sufficient time for this portion of the activity, as the solutions for one to 10 are significantly more difficult. Encourage students to develop a systematic approach to help them solve the puzzle.
4. When all groups have found at least one solution, hand out the fourth student page and allow them to answer the questions.
5. Close with a time of class discussion and sharing where students share their solutions, techniques, and any patterns they discovered in the problem.

**Connecting Learning**
1. How many solutions was your group able to find for the numbers one to six? …the numbers one to 10? [There are four unique solutions for both sets of numbers.]
2. Do you think you found them all? Why or why not?
3. How did you find the answers for the numbers one to six? [Probably trial and error.]
4. When you found the answers for the numbers one to 10, did you use this same approach? Why or why not?
5. What techniques did you use to help you solve the harder problem?
6. What did you notice about the numbers that appeared in the top row of the solutions? [The largest number (either six or 10) must always be in the top row.]
7. Why do you think this is? [No two smaller numbers have a difference that equals the largest number, so the six (or the 10) must always be in the top row.]
8. What other patterns did you notice in the solutions?
9. What other questions did you think of to explore?

**Extensions**
1. Explore the concept of odd and even numbers and how that affects the possible arrangements of numbers in the arrays. Extension pages are provided for this activity.
2. Use other consecutive sets of numbers such as two to 11 or three to 12.
3. Use the numbers one to 15 to make a larger array. (Caution: This array has only one solution and is very difficult.)

**Solutions**
There are four unique solutions for each of the problems (not counting mirror images or solutions where the numbers in a row are simply in a different order).

Using the numbers one to six:

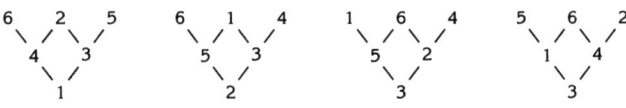

Using the numbers one to 10:

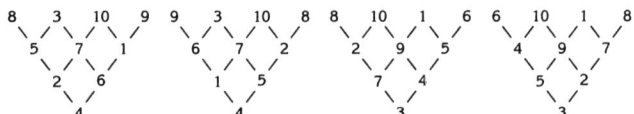

*Unwritten "rules"*
1. One of the first things that students should discover about the arrays is that the largest number must always go in the top row. If it is not in the top row, no solution can be possible, since there are not two numbers that have a difference equivalent to the largest number.
2. In the array using the numbers one to 10, the nine can only go in the top or second row, and if it is in the second row, the one must go next to the 10 in the top row.
3. The larger numbers in the array cannot be in the bottom position.

\* Reprinted with permission from *Principles and Standards for School Mathematics*, 2000 by the National Council of Teachers of Mathematics. All rights reserved.

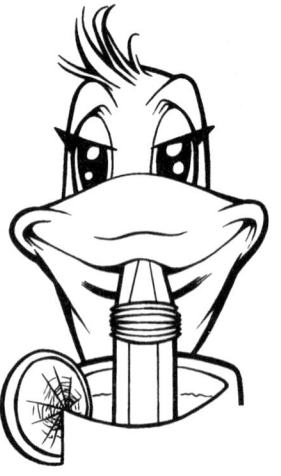

# Making a Difference

**Key Question**

How can you arrange the numbers from one to six in a triangular array so that the difference of any two adjacent numbers appears below those two numbers?

## Learning Goals

### Students will:

- discover how to arrange the numbers from one to six in a triangular array so that each succeeding row is generated by the difference between neighboring numbers from the row above it, and

- be challenged to do the same thing using the numbers one to 10.

# Making a Difference
## PART ONE

Consider the counting numbers one, two, and three. When placed in either of the following triangular arrays, the bottom number is the difference between the two top numbers.

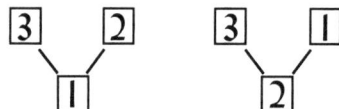

Another way to say that is that each succeeding row is generated by the differences between the neighboring numbers from the row above it. No number is used more than once. You will need to make 10 cards that will fit in the spaces below and number them from one to 10. For this first section, set aside the numbers seven to 10. Your challenge is to use your number cards from one to six and arrange them in the array below so that each number in the bottom two rows is the difference of the two neighboring numbers above it.

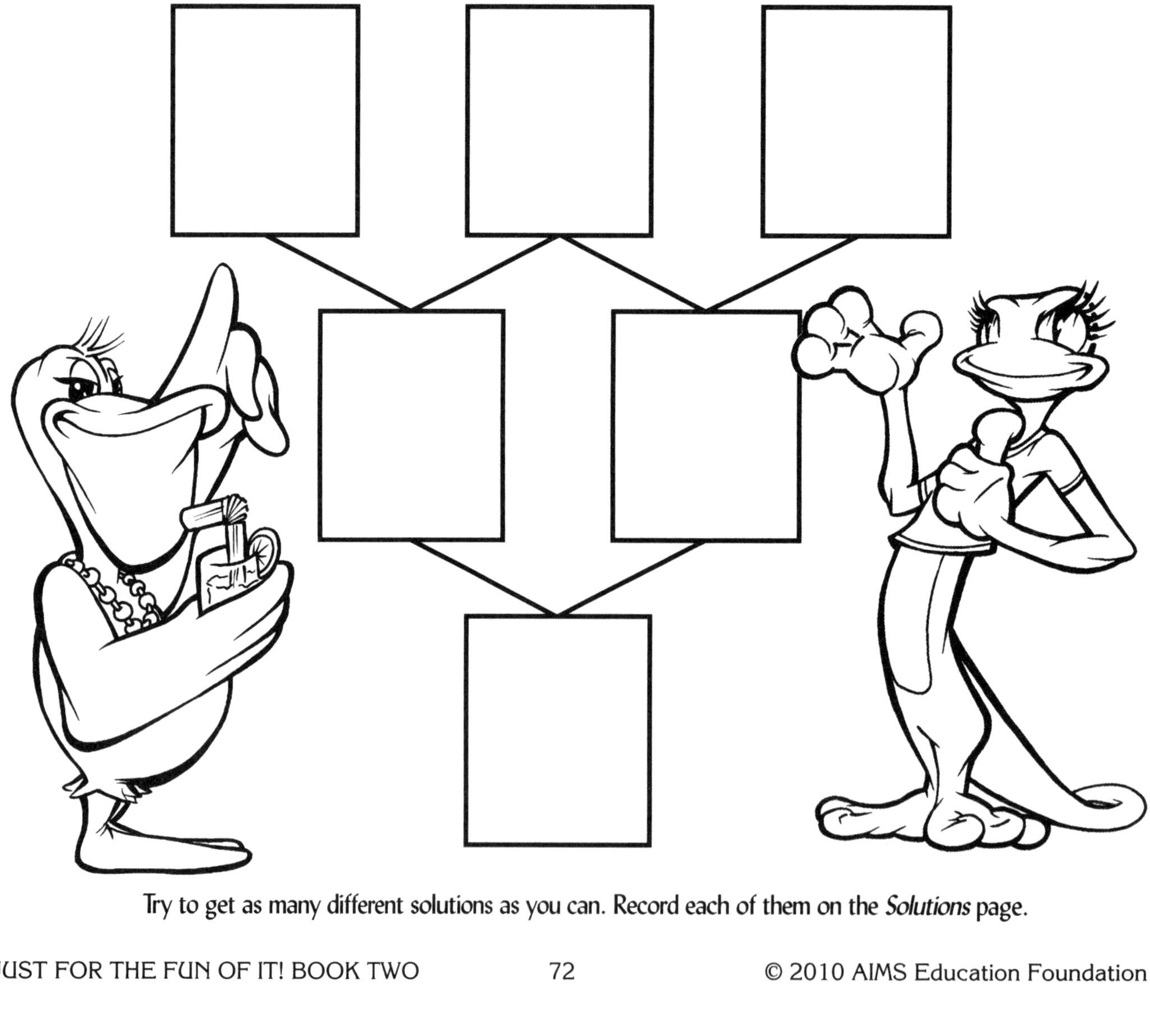

Try to get as many different solutions as you can. Record each of them on the *Solutions* page.

# Making a Difference
## PART TWO

Now that you have found the solutions for the numbers one to six, try to find the solutions using all of your number cards from one to 10. All of the same rules apply that you had in the first challenge.

Record all of your unique solutions on the *Solutions* page.

# Making a Difference SOLUTIONS

# Making a Difference 2

When you have found several solutions for both parts of this activity, answer the questions below.

1. How many solutions were you able to find using the numbers one to six? Do you think you have found them all? Why or why not?

2. How many solutions were you able to find for the numbers one to 10? Do you think you have found them all? Why or why not?

3. Did you notice any patterns or "rules" that you had to follow in order to get a solution? What were they?

4. How did these rules change when you used all of the numbers as opposed to only the first six?

5. List some interesting questions related to this problem that you could explore.

JUST FOR THE FUN OF IT! BOOK TWO

# Making a Difference 2
### Extension

Now that you have discovered the solutions for six and 10 numbers, you are going to study some of the reasons for the arrangement of the solutions. Odd and even numbers have particular characteristics when they are added and subtracted. Complete the chart below indicating what happens when you add and subtract even and odd numbers.

Odd + Odd = _____     Odd − Odd = _____

Odd + Even = _____     Odd − Even = _____

Even + Even = _____     Even − Even = _____

Take your number cards from the main part of the activity and turn them over, writing "odd" or "even" on the back of each card based on the number it has on the other side. You should have five "even" cards, and five "odd" cards. Place the numbers seven to 10 aside for now. Using what you learned from the chart above, arrange the cards in the shape of the six-number array to form the different possible combinations of odd and even numbers. Record all of the unique combinations that you find. Be sure that they are unique even when flipped. One combination has been done for you as an example.

<u>  Even  </u>   <u>  Even  </u>   <u>  Odd  </u>         _____  _____  _____

      <u>  Even  </u>   <u>  Odd  </u>                     _____  _____

           <u>  Odd  </u>                                    _____


_____  _____  _____         _____  _____  _____

   _____  _____                       _____  _____

      _____                                      _____

1. How many unique combinations are possible with three odd and three even numbers?

2. How do you know that you have found them all?

# Making a Difference
## Extension

Take all of the odd and even cards and arrange them in the shape of the 10 number array. Record each unique combination that you discover. One possible combination has been partially filled in for you.

_____ _____ _____ _____      _____ _____ _____ _____

_____ _____ _____          _____ _____

<u> Odd </u>  <u> Odd </u>                _____ _____

<u> Even </u>


_____ _____ _____ _____      _____ _____ _____ _____

_____ _____ _____          _____ _____

_____ _____                    _____

_____

1. How many unique combinations are possible with five odd and five even numbers?

2. How do you know that you have found them all?

3. Why aren't more combinations possible?

4. How would the possibilities be different if there were four even numbers and six odd?

5. How many combinations do you think there would be for seven even and eight odd numbers (the numbers one to 15)? Justify your response.

# Connecting Learning

1. How many solutions was your group able to find for the numbers one to six? …the numbers one to 10?

2. Do you think you found them all? Why or why not?

3. How did you find the answers for the numbers one to six?

4. When you found the answers for the numbers one to 10, did you use this same approach? Why or why not?

# Making a Difference

## Connecting Learning

5. What techniques did you use to help you solve the harder problem?

6. What did you notice about the numbers that appeared in the top row of the solutions?

7. Why do you think this is?

8. What other patterns did you notice in the solutions?

9. What other questions did you think of to explore?

# The Nine-Digit Challenge

**Topic**
Patterns in addition

**Key Question**
What patterns can you discover in this investigation?

**Learning Goals**
Students will:
- use the digits from one to nine to create correct addition problems, and
- explore the patterns present in those problems.

**Guiding Documents**
*Project 2061 Benchmark*
- Mathematics is the study of many kinds of patterns, including numbers and shapes and operations on them. Sometimes patterns are studied because they help to explain how the world works or how to solve practical problems, sometimes because they are interesting in themselves.

*NCTM Standards 2000\**
- Describe, extend, and make generalizations about geometric and numeric patterns
- Build new mathematical knowledge through problem solving

**Math**
Whole number operations
Math patterns
Inductive reasoning
Problem solving

**Integrated Processes**
Observing
Collecting and recording data
Inferring
Relating
Generalizing

**Problem-Solving Strategies**
Guess and check
Look for patterns
Write a number sentence
Organize the information
Use manipulatives

**Materials**
Scratch paper
Bulletin board space or butcher paper
Student pages

**Background Information**
This problem differs from the others in this book in that it has an independent section, a group-work section, and a whole-class section. The *Nine-Digit Challenge* is designed to tap into several areas such as basic computation, pattern recognition, and problem solving. It can be used over a period of several days to a week and presents the opportunity to develop several beneficial skills with one basic problem. In addition to applying basic mathematical skills, this activity is designed to be used as a class project by creating a wall of solutions where students will display their individual work and the class can work together to discover all 336 solutions.

**Management**
1. This problem consists of three parts and may be most effective if done over a period of several days. The first section uses student pages one and two and requires students to work independently to discover as many solutions as possible to the addition problem. This part may be done over the course of a week, with students finding solutions in their spare time, or in a time set aside to work on the problem. You may wish to devote a center to solution discovery. The second section uses student page three and has students record each unique solution they discover and put it on the wall of solutions in an attempt to discover all 336 solutions as a class. The third section uses student pages four and five and has students work in groups to discover the patterns in the solutions they have found. This part should be done all at one time, not spread over several days.
2. Each student will need to make his or her own set of number cards (one to nine) to use in the first part of the problem. The easiest way to do this is to have them cut up scratch paper and write the numbers on the cards. The cards should fit into the spaces on the first student page (about 3 cm x 4.5 cm). Small sticky notes will also work.

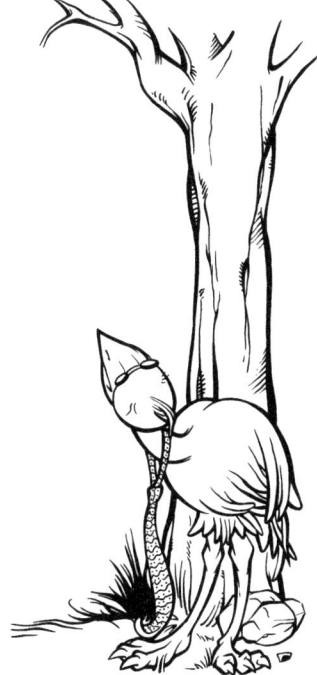

3. Since there are 336 different solutions to this problem, you may want to have extra copies of the solutions page (page two) for students who discover more than 16 solutions.
4. To create a wall of solutions, you will need some bulletin board space, or a similar area where students can post the solutions they discover. Student page three is for this part of the activity. This page can be photocopied, cut into fourths and left out for students to use as they discover solutions. The biggest challenge of the wall of solutions is monitoring the solutions so that there are no duplicates posted. The students can be responsible for this monitoring, or you may wish to do it yourself. One of the advantages of using this approach is that the "data" (solutions) can be moved around on the board allowing them to be organized in various ways.

## Procedure
1. Have the students make their sets of number cards from one to nine.
2. Distribute student pages one and two and review the instructions. *Using the number cards you have made, place them in the spaces on your paper to produce a correct addition problem. Each problem requires you to carry an "invisible" one, but this one is not counted as one of the nine digits.*
3. Have students work alone to find as many valid solutions as they can (either over the course of several days, or in one period).
4. Explain the guidelines for the wall of solutions and make the solution recording papers available to students. When students find solutions, have them write the solutions on their own record pages as well as add them to the wall (if they have not already been discovered by someone else).
5. When each student has had sufficient time to find at least one solution on his or her own, divide the class into groups and hand out student pages four and five.
6. After all groups have completed the problem, regroup for a time of class discussion where groups can share the patterns they discovered.

## Connecting Learning
To facilitate discussion, lead the class through the answers to the questions on student page five, having students share the patterns they discovered where it is appropriate.
1. What is the sum of the digits in each sum? [18]
2. What is the largest possible sum? [981] How do you know? [It is the largest number in this activity with digits that add to 18.]
3. What are all the possible sums greater than 900? [981, 972, 963, 954, 945, 936, 927, and 918] What patterns do you notice in this sequence? [The digits all have a sum of 18, as the ones place digit goes up by one, the tens place digit goes down by one, etc.]
4. What are all the possible sums greater than 800 and less than 900? [891, 873, 864, 846, 837, and 819] Why does this list have fewer numbers than the list of sums greater than 900? [Several sums whose digits total 18 (882, 855, and 828) are missing from this sequence because of the repeating digits.]
5. What are all the possible sums greater than 700 and less than 800? [792, 783, 765, 756, 738, and 729] For which numbers in this list are no solutions possible? [765, 765]
6. What is the smallest possible sum? Give an example of a problem with this sum. [The smallest possible sum is not 189, as the pattern might suggest. Students should be encouraged to verbalize why this is so (there are two digits being added in the hundreds place and they cannot equal one hundred). While there might be a possible sum in the 300s according to the pattern (387 or 396 for example), students will find that these sums do not work. The smallest possible sum that produces a correct addition problem is 459 (173 + 286).]
7. For any given sum, several different problems can be obtained by switching around the digits in the top and middle rows. How many different problems are there for each sum? List all the problems for one sum. [For any given sum there are either eight or 16 different problems that can be obtained by switching around the numbers in the addends. For example, 657 + 324, 654 + 327, 627 + 354, 624 + 357, 357 + 624, 354 + 627, 327 + 654, and 324 + 657 all produce 981 as a sum.]
8. What additional patterns did you discover? (See *Solutions*.)

## Extensions
1. Solve the problem using subtraction instead of addition. (*Extension One* gives some spaces in which to record those solutions.)
2. Add three two-digit numbers to get a three-digit answer. (*Extension Two* provides a template for this.)
3. Use the numbers zero to eight instead of one to nine.
   For example:   326
   $\underline{+\ 178}$
   504
4. Modify student page one to accommodate a four-digit answer, and use 10 digits—zero to nine.
   For example:   432
   $\underline{+\ 657}$
   1089

Solutions

One of the first things that students should discover when doing this problem is that the digits in the sums always add up to 18. There are 11 three-number combinations that have a sum of 18 (assuming each number is one digit). Each of these combinations can be arranged to make a variety of numbers, as shown.

| Three-number combinations that total 18 | Values that can be made using these numbers |
|---|---|
| 1, 8, 9 | 189, 198, 819, 891, 918, 981 |
| 2, 7, 9 | 279, 297, 729, 792, 927, 972 |
| 2, 8, 8 | 288, 828, 882 |
| 3, 6, 9 | 369, 396, 639, 693, 936, 963 |
| 3, 7, 8 | 378, 387, 738, 783, 837, 873 |
| 4, 5, 9 | 459, 495, 549, 594, 945, 954 |
| 4, 6, 8 | 468, 486, 648, 684, 846, 864 |
| 4, 7, 7 | 477, 747, 774 |
| 5, 5, 8 | 558, 585, 855 |
| 5, 6, 7 | 567, 576, 657, 675, 756, 765 |
| 6, 6, 6 | 666 |

If those numbers with repeating digits are eliminated, a list of theoretically possible sums can be constructed.

**Theoretically Possible Sums**

| 981 | 891 | 792 | 693 | 594 | 495 | 396 | 297 | 198 |
|---|---|---|---|---|---|---|---|---|
| 972 | 873 | 783 | 684 | 576 | 486 | 387 | 279 | 189 |
| 963 | 864 | 765 | 675 | 567 | 468 | 378 | | |
| 954 | 846 | 756 | 657 | 549 | 459 | 369 | | |
| 945 | 837 | 738 | 648 | | | | | |
| 936 | 819 | 729 | 639 | | | | | |
| 927 | | | | | | | | |
| 918 | | | | | | | | |

Of these 42 theoretically possible sums, 11 are not possible. Eight are not possible because they are so small that workable addition problem cannot be created using the large numbers that are left over. These numbers are: 396, 387, 378, 369, 297, 279, 198, and 189.

The remaining three impossible sums simply cannot be done. For some reason, sums of 765, 756, and 684 cannot be created within the limits of this problem. Taking all of this into account, there are 31 actual possible sums, with the largest being 981, and the smallest being 459.

**Actual Possible Sums**

981 972 963 954 945 936 927 918
891 873 864 846 837 819
792 783 738 729
693 675 657 648 639
594 576 567 549
486 495 468 459

One possible way to create each sum is shown below.

**Nine-Digit Sums**

| 327 | 658 | 218 | 283 | 628 | 784 | 586 | 645 | 267 | 654 | 291 |
|---|---|---|---|---|---|---|---|---|---|---|
| + 654 | + 314 | + 745 | + 671 | + 317 | + 152 | + 341 | + 273 | + 645 | + 219 | + 573 |
| 981 | 972 | 963 | 954 | 945 | 936 | 927 | 918 | 891 | 873 | 864 |

| 529 | 692 | 273 | 638 | 269 | 592 | 583 | 215 | 183 | 418 | 391 |
|---|---|---|---|---|---|---|---|---|---|---|
| + 317 | + 145 | + 546 | + 154 | + 514 | + 146 | + 146 | + 478 | + 492 | + 239 | + 257 |
| 846 | 837 | 819 | 792 | 783 | 738 | 729 | 693 | 675 | 657 | 648 |

| 152 | 218 | 182 | 219 | 382 | 328 | 327 | 295 | 176 |
|---|---|---|---|---|---|---|---|---|
| + 487 | + 376 | + 394 | + 348 | + 167 | + 167 | + 159 | + 173 | + 283 |
| 639 | 594 | 576 | 567 | 549 | 495 | 486 | 468 | 459 |

There are at least eight combinations that will yield each of the possible sums. In all of these combinations, the numbers in the vertical columns remain constant, they are simply flip-flopped one at a time to create different horizontal combinations. For example:

| 152 | 157 | 182 | 187 | 482 | 487 | 452 | 457 |
|---|---|---|---|---|---|---|---|
| + 487 | + 482 | + 457 | + 452 | + 157 | + 152 | + 187 | + 182 |
| 639 | 639 | 639 | 639 | 639 | 639 | 639 | 639 |

As you can see, the four is always with the one, the five is always with the eight, and the two is always with the seven.

The example above works with all 31 sums, but there are 11 sums that have a total of 16 variations instead of eight. These sums are:
981 954 945 918 891 864 837 819 783 675 567

In six of these cases, the extra variations occur because there are two vertical columns that have the same sum. Therefore, the columns can be switched, and a whole new set of numbers created to reach the sum. For example:

```
  269        629
+ 514      + 154
  783        783
```

In the first problem above, there are two vertical columns that total 7: 2 + 5 and 6 + 1. If these columns are reversed, the result is the problem on the right, which still yields the same sum. Both of these problems have eight variations, giving a total of 16 ways to create 783. The other numbers that follow this same pattern are 837, 918, 891, 675, and 567.

There are five sums that have 16 variations, but for a different reason than those just mentioned. In these five cases, it is possible to get the same sum with two different pairings of the numbers. Instead of keeping the vertical columns constant (two is always with five, six is always with nine, etc.), they are mixed, but still create the same sum. For example:

$$\begin{array}{r} 238 \\ +716 \\ \hline 954 \end{array} \qquad \begin{array}{r} 283 \\ +671 \\ \hline 954 \end{array}$$

In the first problem, two is with seven, three is with one, and eight is with six. In the second problem, two is with six, three is with one, and eight is with seven. Again, both of these problems have eight variations, giving a total of 16 ways to create 954. The other numbers that follow this same pattern are 981, 945, 864, and 819. This information is summarized in the table below.

| Sums that have 8 combinations | Sums that have 16 combinations |
|---|---|
| 972 963 936 927 | 981 954 945 918 |
| 873 864 846 837 | 891 864 837 819 |
| 792 738 729 | 783 675 567 |
| 693 657 648 639 | |
| 594 576 549 | |
| 495 486 468 459 | |

With all of the different variations and possible sums, there are a total of 336 different solutions to the *Nine-Digit Challenge*.

```
  20 sums with eight combinations = 160 solutions
+ 11 sums with 16 combinations    = 176 solutions
                            Total = 336 solutions
```

\* Reprinted with permission from *Principles and Standards for School Mathematics*, 2000 by the National Council of Teachers of Mathematics. All rights reserved.

# The Nine-Digit Challenge

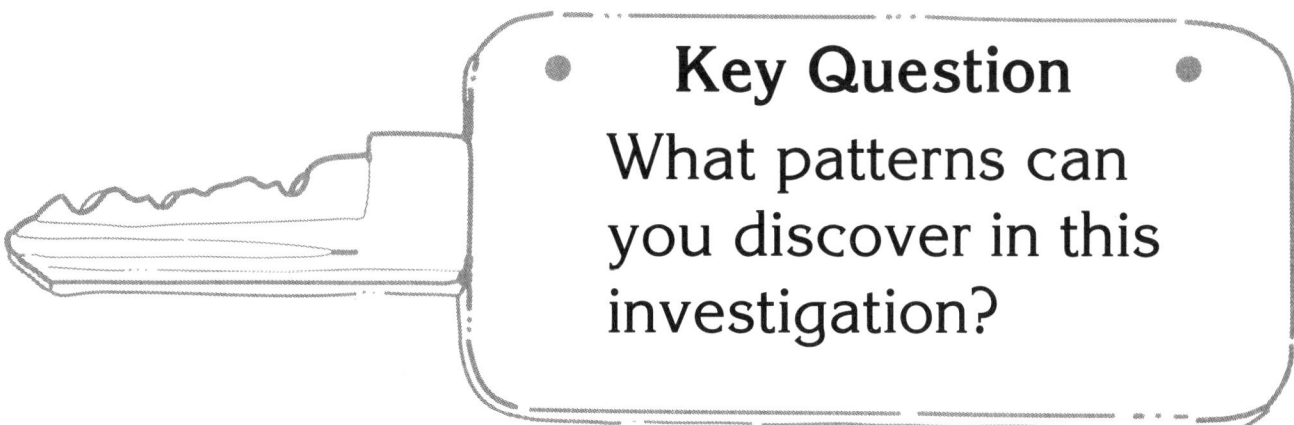

**Key Question**

What patterns can you discover in this investigation?

## Learning Goals

**Students will:**

- use the digits from one to nine to create correct addition problems, and

- explore the patterns present in those problems.

# The Nine-Digit Challenge

Using a piece of scratch paper, cut out nine rectangular cards that will fit in the boxes below. Number the cards from one to nine. Use them in the spaces below to produce a correct addition problem. Each problem will require you to carry an "invisible" one, but this one is not counted as one of the nine digits. Record your solutions on the next page. Try to get as many solutions as possible. (There are over 300!)

JUST FOR THE FUN OF IT! BOOK TWO © 2010 AIMS Education Foundation

# The Nine-Digit Challenge

Record your solutions in the spaces below.

JUST FOR THE FUN OF IT! BOOK TWO

Name: _____

Name: _____

Name: _____

Name: _____

# The Nine-Digit Challenge

Get together with your group and study your solutions. Share any patterns, insights, or ways of finding solutions that you discovered with your group. Work together and answer the following questions.

1. What patterns did you discover in this activity?

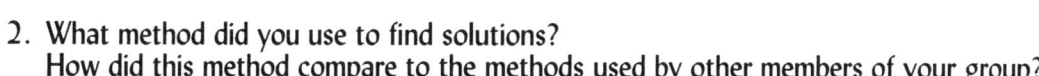

2. What method did you use to find solutions?
   How did this method compare to the methods used by other members of your group?

3. Did you or any member of your group find any short cuts?
   If so, describe them.

4. What insights did your group have about this problem?

JUST FOR THE FUN OF IT! BOOK TWO

# The Nine-Digit Challenge

You may have noticed that the sum in each nine-digit problem is special. The following questions will help focus your mathematical thinking. Use the back of the paper if you need more space.

1. What is special about all the sums?

2. What is the largest possible sum? How do you know?

3. List all the possible sums greater than 900.

4. List all the possible sums greater than 800 and less than 900.

5. List all the possible sums greater than 700 and less than 800.
   Two of these answers fit the pattern but do not work. Can you find them?

6. What is the smallest possible sum? Show a problem with this sum.

7. For any given sum, several different problems can be obtained by switching around the digits in the top and middle rows. How many different problems is it possible to have for each sum?
   Choose one sum and show all the problems.

8. What additional patterns did you discover while answering the above questions?

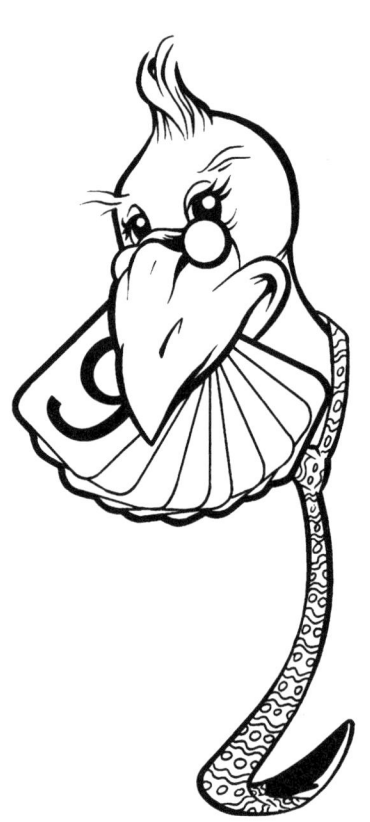

# The Nine-Digit Challenge
## Extension #1

Use the digits one to nine to create correct subtraction problems. Record your solutions in the spaces below.

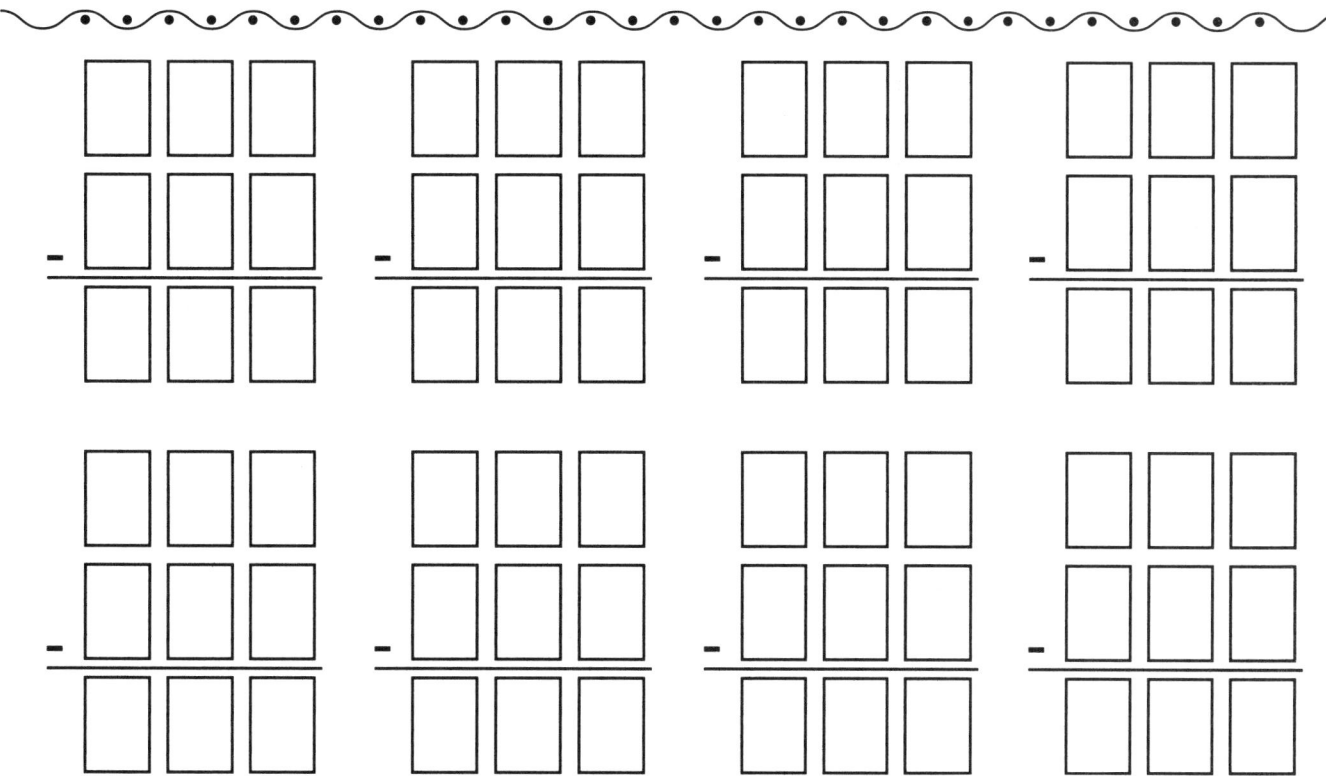

Describe some of the things you notice about your solutions in the space below.

# The Nine-Digit Challenge
## Extension #2

Place the numbers one to nine in the spaces below so that they form a correct addition problem.

# The Nine-Digit Challenge

## Connecting Learning

1. What is the sum of the digits in each sum?

2. What is the largest possible sum? How do you know?

3. What are all the possible sums greater than 900? What patterns do you notice in this sequence?

4. What are all the possible sums greater than 800 and less than 900? Why does this list have fewer numbers than the list of sums greater than 900?

5. What are all the possible sums greater than 700 and less than 800? For which numbers in this list are no solutions possible?

# The Nine-Digit Challenge

## Connecting Learning

6. What is the smallest possible sum? Give an example of a problem with this sum.

7. For any given sum, several different problems can be obtained by switching around the digits in the top and middle rows. How many different problems are there for each sum? List all the problems for one sum.

8. What additional patterns did you discover?

# Eight-Digit Addition

**Topic**
Patterns in addition

**Key Question**
What patterns can you discover as you create correct addition problems using the digits from one to eight, two to nine, and zero to seven?

**Learning Goals**
Students will:
* use the numbers from one to eight, two to nine, and zero to seven to create correct addition problems; and
* search for patterns in their solutions.

**Guiding Documents**
*Project 2061 Benchmark*
* *Mathematics is the study of many kinds of patterns, including numbers and shapes and operations on them. Sometimes patterns are studied because they help to explain how the world works or how to solve practical problems, sometimes because they are interesting in themselves.*

*NCTM Standards 2000\**
* *Describe, extend, and make generalizations about geometric and numeric patterns*
* *Build new mathematical knowledge through problem solving*

**Math**
Whole number operations
Math patterns
Problem solving

**Integrated Processes**
Observing
Comparing and contrasting
Generalizing

**Problem-Solving Strategies**
Look for patterns
Write a number sentence
Guess and check
Organize the information
Use manipulatives

**Materials**
Scratch paper
Student pages

**Background Information**
This activity is closely related to the *Nine-Digit Challenge*, and can be done in conjunction with that activity. Instead of creating a three-digit sum by adding two three-digit numbers, *Eight-Digit Addition* challenges students to create a three-digit sum by adding a two-digit number and a three-digit number. This variation necessitates an "invisible" one being carried to the hundreds place. A problem that does not do this will not work because the digit in the hundreds place of the top number and the hundreds place of the sum would be the same. Since there is only one of each number, this is not possible. Like the *Nine-Digit Challenge*, this activity allows students to practice their basic computational skills while simultaneously working on their problem-solving skills and pattern-discovery abilities.

**Management**
1. Students will each need number cards from zero to nine. These cards can be easily made from scratch paper that has been cut into rectangles about the size of the spaces on the student page (about 3 cm x 4.5 cm). Small sticky notes will also work. If students still have their number cards from *The Nine-Digit Challenge*, they will only need to make a number card for zero.
2. You will want to have extra copies of the solutions page on hand since there are many more solutions possible than spaces available.
3. If you are doing this activity in conjunction with the *Nine-Digit Challenge*, it is recommended that you do this activity second, since it is the more difficult of the two.
4. As mentioned above, students will need to carry an "invisible" one to the hundreds place in order to arrive at a correct solution. The one is "invisible" because it does not count as one of the eight digits that students use in the problem. It is important that students know that they are allowed to carry an invisible one before they attempt to discover any solutions.

**Procedure**
1. If necessary, distribute scratch paper and have students create their number cards, labeling them from zero to nine.
2. Hand out student pages one and two and have students work in small groups to discover as many solutions as they can using the numbers one to eight, two to nine, and zero to seven.

JUST FOR THE FUN OF IT! BOOK TWO     95     © 2010 AIMS Education Foundation

3. When all groups have had sufficient time to discover several solutions for each set of numbers, hand out the third student page and have students answer the questions.
4. Close with a time of class discussion where students share their solutions as well as the patterns that they discovered.

**Connecting Learning**
1. How many solutions did you discover for the numbers one to eight? ...two to nine? ...zero to seven?
2. How many solutions do you think there actually are for each of those sets of numbers? [There are 16 for one to eight and two to nine, and there are eight for zero to seven.]
3. What is the smallest sum you were able to get? [230 is the smallest possible sum, using the numbers zero to seven.] ...the largest? [823 is the largest possible sum, using the numbers two to nine.]
4. What patterns did you see in your solutions? (See *Solutions*.)
5. How do the patterns compare between the sets of numbers? (See *Solutions*.)

**Extension**
Change the problem to subtraction instead of addition. An extension page has been provided for this purpose.

**Solutions**
Each solution for the three different sets of numbers is shown here. A discussion of some of the patterns follows.

*One to eight*

| 178 | 176 | 158 | 156 |
|---|---|---|---|
| + 56 | + 58 | + 76 | + 78 |
| 234 | 234 | 234 | 234 |

| 267 | 268 | 247 | 248 |
|---|---|---|---|
| + 48 | + 47 | + 68 | + 67 |
| 315 | 315 | 315 | 315 |

| 487 | 486 | 427 | 426 |
|---|---|---|---|
| + 26 | + 27 | + 86 | + 87 |
| 513 | 513 | 513 | 513 |

| 587 | 584 | 537 | 534 |
|---|---|---|---|
| + 34 | + 37 | + 84 | + 87 |
| 621 | 621 | 621 | 621 |

*Two to nine*

| 287 | 289 | 257 | 259 |
|---|---|---|---|
| + 59 | + 57 | + 89 | + 87 |
| 346 | 346 | 346 | 346 |

| 369 | 368 | 359 | 358 |
|---|---|---|---|
| + 58 | + 59 | + 68 | + 69 |
| 427 | 427 | 427 | 427 |

| 483 | 489 | 473 | 479 |
|---|---|---|---|
| + 79 | + 73 | + 89 | + 83 |
| 562 | 562 | 562 | 562 |

| 769 | 764 | 759 | 754 |
|---|---|---|---|
| + 54 | + 59 | + 64 | + 69 |
| 823 | 823 | 823 | 823 |

*Zero to seven*

| 156 | 154 | 176 | 174 |
|---|---|---|---|
| + 74 | + 76 | + 54 | + 56 |
| 230 | 230 | 230 | 230 |

| 375 | 376 | 325 | 326 |
|---|---|---|---|
| + 26 | + 25 | + 76 | + 75 |
| 401 | 401 | 230 | 230 |

*Patterns*
- You must carry a one to the hundreds place in each problem, making the first digit in the sum one more than the first digit in the top addend.
- For the numbers one to eight, the numbers that make up the sum always add up to nine. For example, 2 + 3 + 4 = 9, 3 + 1 + 5 = 9, and 6 + 2 + 1 = 9.
- For the numbers two to nine, the numbers that make up the sum always add up to 13. For example, 3 + 4 + 6 = 13, 4 + 2 + 7 = 13, 5 + 6 + 2 = 13, and 8 + 2 + 3 = 13.
- For the numbers zero to seven, the numbers that make up the sum always add up to five. For example, 2 + 3 + 0 = 5 and 4 + 0 + 1 = 5.
- For the numbers one to eight and two to nine, there are four different sums that are possible. The five digits that make up the top numbers in each problem can be arranged a total of four different ways to produce the same sum. This results in a total of 16 unique solutions for each of these sets of numbers.
- For the numbers zero to seven, there are only two different sums possible, for a total of eight unique solutions.

\* Reprinted with permission from *Principles and Standards for School Mathematics*, 2000 by the National Council of Teachers of Mathematics. All rights reserved.

# Eight-Digit Addition

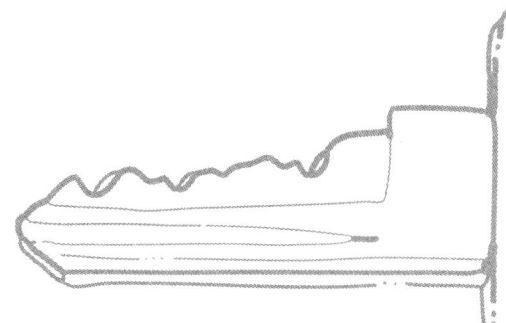

**Key Question**

What patterns can you discover as you create correct addition problems using the digits from one to eight, two to nine, and zero to seven?

## Learning Goals

### Students will:

- use the numbers from one to eight, two to nine, and zero to seven to create correct addition problems; and

- search for patterns in their solutions.

# Eight-Digit Addition

Place your number cards from one to eight in the spaces below so that they form a correct addition problem.

**Extra Challenge:** When you have found as many solutions as you can using the numbers one to eight, try using the numbers two to nine and zero to seven.

# Eight-Digit Addition

Record your solutions in the spaces below. If you need more spaces, ask your teacher for another solutions page.

# Eight-Digit Addition

When you have found several solutions for the numbers one to eight, zero to seven, and two to nine, answer the questions below.

1. How many solutions did you find using the numbers one to eight? Do you think you have them all? Why or why not?

2. How many different sums were you able to get? What do you notice about these sums?

3. How many different ways were you able to get each sum? Why?

4. What was different about the solutions you got using the numbers zero to seven and two to nine?

5. What was the same?

6. What patterns do you see in this problem?

# Eight-Digit Addition

Place your number cards from one to eight in the spaces below so that they form a correct subtraction problem.

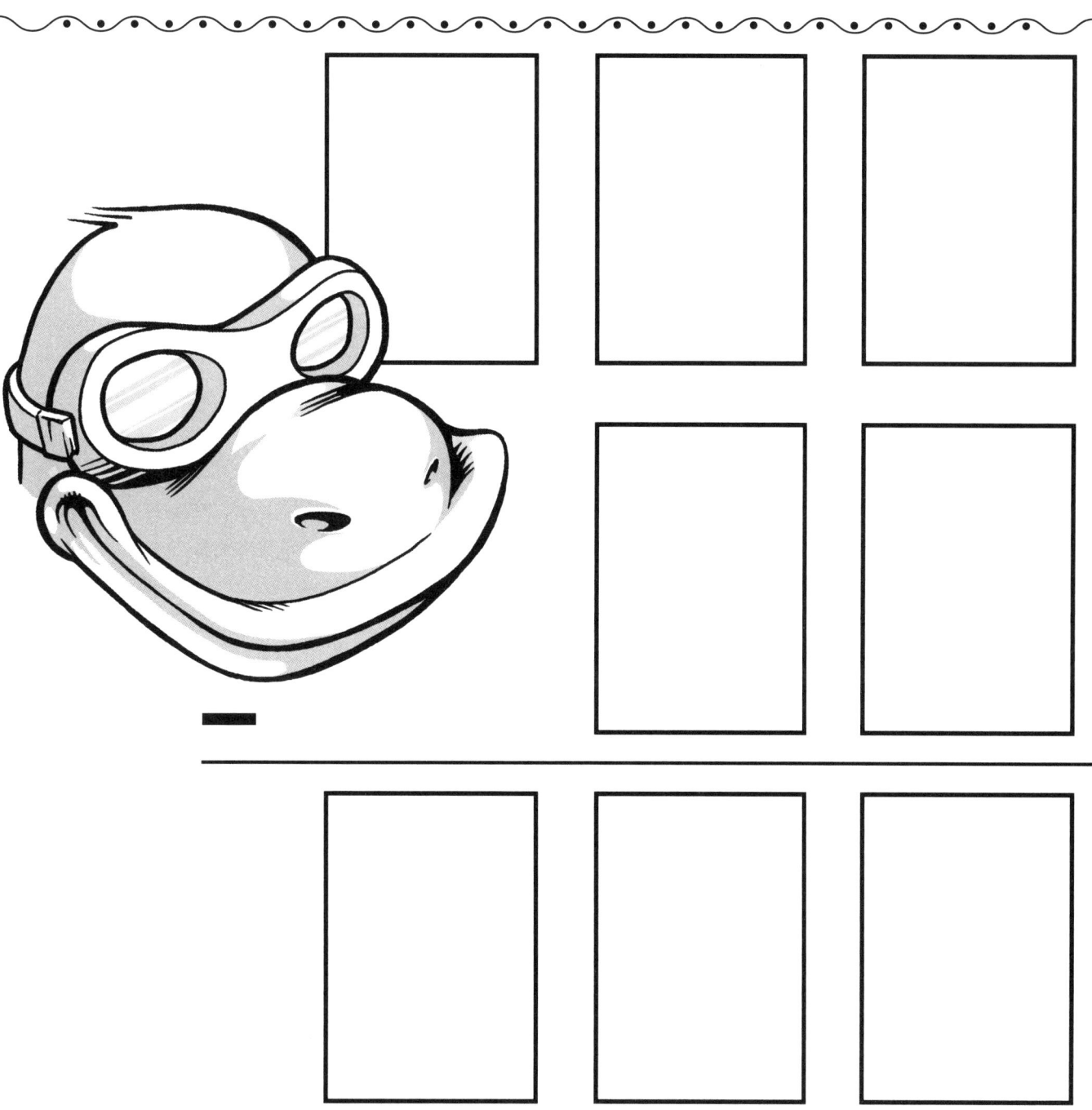

**Extra Challenge:** When you have found as many solutions as you can using the numbers one to eight, try using the numbers two to nine and zero to seven..

# Eight-Digit Addition

Record your solutions in the spaces below. If you need more spaces, ask your teacher for another solutions page.

# Eight-Digit Addition

## Connecting Learning

1. How many solutions did you discover for the numbers one to eight? …two to nine? …zero to seven?

2. How many solutions do you think there actually are for each of those sets of numbers?

3. What is the smallest sum you were able to get? …the largest?

4. What patterns did you see in your solutions?

5. How do the patterns compare between the sets of numbers?

# Side by Side

**Topic**
Perimeter and area

**Key Question**
What patterns do you see in the perimeters and areas of squares with sides ranging from one to nine units in length?

**Learning Goal**
Students will discover some interesting patterns as they explore the relationships between the sides, perimeters, and areas of unit squares.

**Guiding Documents**
*Project 2061 Benchmarks*
- Length can be thought of a unit lengths joined together, and area as a collection of unit squares.
- Organize information in simple tables and graphs and identify relationships they reveal.
- Graphical display of numbers may make it possible to spot patterns that are not otherwise obvious.
- Mathematics is the study of many kinds of patterns, including numbers and shapes and operations on them. Sometimes patterns are studied because they help to explain how the world works or how to solve practical problems, sometimes because they are interesting in themselves.

*NCTM Standards 2000\**
- Describe, extend, and make generalizations about geometric and numeric patterns
- Represent and analyze patterns and functions using words, tables, and graphs
- Explore what happens to measurements of a two-dimensional shape such as its perimeter and area when the shape is changed in some way
- Understand relationships among the side lengths, perimeters and areas of similar objects
- Build new mathematical knowledge through problem solving

**Math**
Measurement
 perimeter
 area
Graphing
 line graphs
Math patterns
Problem solving

**Integrated Processes**
Observing
Collecting and recording data
Interpreting data
Comparing and contrasting
Relating

**Problem-Solving Strategies**
Organize the information
Look for patterns

**Materials**
Colored pens or pencils
Student pages
Geoboards and rubber bands, optional

**Background Information**
This activity allows students to deepen their understanding of the concepts of perimeter and area, but should not be used as an introduction to those concepts. *Side by Side* takes an in-depth look at the relationship between perimeter and area in squares of different sizes. Students will compare these values by entering them in a table and creating a line graph. Both of these methods will help them to better understand the relationship between perimeter and area. Students will also improve their pattern-recognition skills as they search for the patterns that exist in both the perimeter and area individually as well as in relation to each other.

**Management**
1. This activity should not be used as an introduction to perimeter, area, or graphing. Students should already be comfortable with these concepts before attempting *Side by Side*.
2. Instead of having students color in unit squares on the grid paper, you may wish to have them use geoboards and colored rubber bands for this task.

JUST FOR THE FUN OF IT! BOOK TWO

## Procedure
1. Hand out the student pages (and geoboards, if desired) and go over the instructions. *On a piece of grid paper (your geoboard) color in unit squares with sides of one, two, three, four, five, six, seven, eight, and nine. Find the perimeter of each square and record it in the chart. Make a line graph of the perimeter as it relates to side length. Next, find the area of each square. Record this data in the chart. Graph this line in a different color.*
2. Have students work together in small groups to fill in the table and create the graph.
3. When all groups have had time to discover several patterns, close with a time of class discussion where students share their discoveries.

## Connecting Learning
1. What patterns did you see in the perimeters? [They always increase by four, their graph forms a straight line, etc.]
2. What patterns did you see in the areas? [The areas are always square numbers, their graph forms a curve, etc.]
3. What things do you notice about the relationship between perimeter and area? [Area increases much faster than perimeter, the lines on the graph cross at 16, etc.]
4. How did the graph help you to recognize the patterns that exist?

## Extensions
1. Have students find and graph the volume of unit cubes with sides from one to nine units long and compare these values to the perimeter and area values.
2. Challenge students to develop perimeter and area formulas for squares based on what they have learned.

## Solutions
The solutions contain the table from the first student page as well as the graph of the perimeter and the area. The values for volume have been added to the table, as well as a generalization for each formula.

| Length of Side | 1 | 2 | 3 | 4 | 5 | 6 | 7 | 8 | 9 | $n$ |
|---|---|---|---|---|---|---|---|---|---|---|
| Perimeter | 4 | 8 | 12 | 16 | 20 | 24 | 28 | 32 | 36 | $4n$ |
| Area | 1 | 4 | 9 | 16 | 25 | 36 | 49 | 64 | 81 | $n^2$ |
| Volume | 1 | 8 | 27 | 64 | 125 | 216 | 343 | 512 | 729 | $n^3$ |

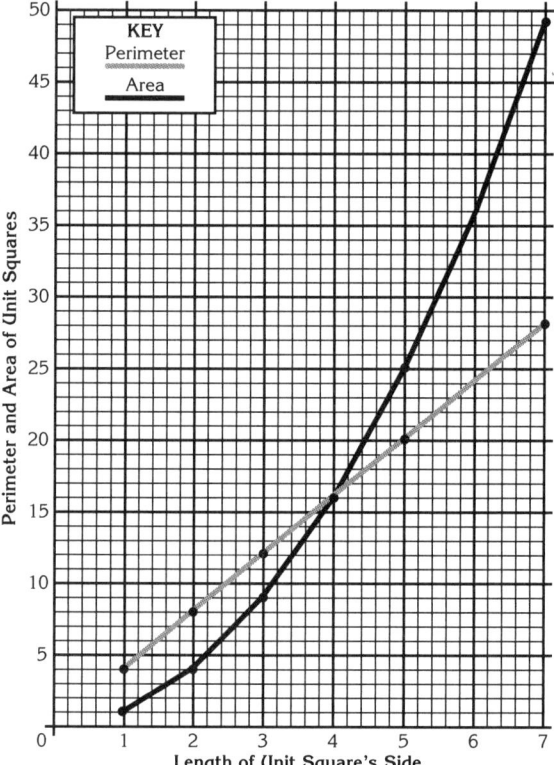

\* Reprinted with permission from *Principles and Standards for School Mathematics*, 2000 by the National Council of Teachers of Mathematics. All rights reserved.

## Key Question

What patterns do you see in the perimeters and areas of squares with sides ranging from one to nine units in length?

## Learning Goal

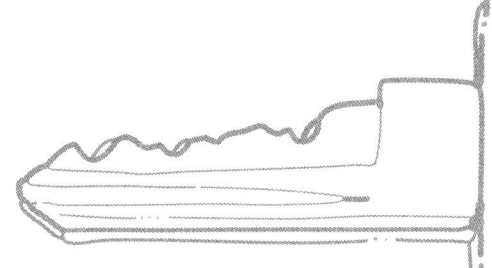

discover some interesting patterns as they explore the relationships between the sides, perimeters, and areas of unit squares.

On your piece of grid paper, color in unit squares with sides of one, two, three, four, five, six, seven, eight, and nine. Find the perimeter and area of each square and record these values in the table below. On the next page, make a line graph of the perimeter values as they relate to side length and the area values as they relate to side length. Use a different color for each of the two lines.

| Length of Side | 1 | 2 | 3 | 4 | 5 | 6 | 7 | 8 | 9 |
|---|---|---|---|---|---|---|---|---|---|
| Perimeter | | | | | | | | | |
| Area | | | | | | | | | |

What patterns do you notice in the table?

What patterns do you notice in the graph on the following page?

# Side by Side

Graph the first seven perimeter and area values as they relate to the length of the side of each square. Draw each line in a different color, recording the color in the appropriate space in the key.

KEY
Perimeter _____
Area _____

*y-axis:* Perimeter and Area of Unit Squares (0 to 50)
*x-axis:* Length of Unit Square's Side (0 to 7)

JUST FOR THE FUN OF IT! BOOK TWO © 2010 AIMS Education Foundation

## Connecting Learning

1. What patterns did you see in the perimeters?

2. What patterns did you see in the areas?

3. What things do you notice about the relationship between perimeter and area?

4. How did the graph help you to recognize the patterns that exist?

# Looking for a Liter

**Topic**
Volume

**Key Question**
What are the dimensions of some cartons that would hold a liter?

**Learning Goals**
Students will:
* explore volume by finding the dimensions of several cartons that would hold one liter, and
* determine which is the most efficient shape by comparing the surface areas of the different cartons.

**Guiding Documents**
*Project 2061 Benchmark*
* *Organize information in simple tables and identify relationships they reveal.*

*NCTM Standards 2000\**
* *Develop strategies to determine the surface areas and volumes of rectangular solids*
* *Build new mathematical knowledge through problem solving*
* *Create and use representations to organize, record, and communicate mathematical ideas*

**Math**
Whole number operations
Measurement
    volume
    surface area, optional
Problem solving

**Integrated Processes**
Observing
Predicting
Collecting and recording data
Comparing and contrasting
Interpreting data
Generalizing

**Problem-Solving Strategies**
Organize the information
Look for patterns

**Materials**
Student pages

**Background Information**
The metric system, which is used most places outside the United States, uses the liter as its standard unit of liquid measurement. This activity combines a study of volume with an opportunity for students to practice working in the metric system. Students are challenged to find the dimensions of at least five cartons that have a volume of one liter. There is also the opportunity to extend this activity to include surface area and to discuss what makes containers efficient.

**Management**
1. Students will need to have a well-developed conceptual understanding of volume before doing this activity—*Looking for a Liter* only deals with volume at an abstract level. They should also know how to calculate volume of a rectangular prism by multiplying its length, width, and height.
2. Students should be familiar with metric units and know that a liter is equal to 1000 milliliters (mL) and that each milliliter is equal to one cubic centimeter ($cm^3$).
3. Both an open-ended and a structured approach are provided for this activity. Determine which method is best for your class and hand out the appropriate student page. The first student page is for the open-ended approach, and the second is for the structured approach.
4. A third student page is provided that takes students through surface area calculations to determine the most efficient carton. Depending on the level of your class or what you want to accomplish with this activity, you may choose to eliminate this page.

**Procedure**
1. Hand out student page one or two and go over the instructions with the class. *Find the dimensions of at least five other cartons that would hold one liter.*
2. Have students work together in small groups to determine the dimensions of at least five other cartons. Be sure that they predict which carton is the most efficient and justify their responses.

JUST FOR THE FUN OF IT! BOOK TWO     113     © 2010 AIMS Education Foundation

3. If desired, hand out the third student page so that students can determine the surface areas of each of their cartons. Be sure that they understand the procedure for determining total surface area.
4. When all groups have finished, close with a time of class discussion where students share the dimensions they discovered and the predictions they made.

## Connecting Learning
1. What are some of the dimensions you were able to find that would hold one liter? (See *Solutions*.)
2. Which of these cartons would be the most efficient? [The 10 x 10 x 10 carton is the most efficient.] Why? [It has the smallest surface area.]
3. How is surface area related to the efficiency of the carton? [The smaller the surface area, the fewer materials needed to construct the carton, increasing efficiency.]
4. Why does the 10 x 10 x 10 carton have the smallest surface area? [A cube always has the smallest surface area when dealing with multiple rectangular prism cartons that have the same volume.]
5. What does this knowledge about surface area tell you about the various cartons you see and use on a daily basis? [Often cartons do not have the most efficient dimensions based on the volume they hold.]

## Extensions
1. Have students bring in various cartons from home and compare their efficiency based on volume and surface area calculations.
2. Determine the most efficient carton for a volume of 1500 cm³ or 800 cm³ if side values must be in whole units.
3. Find all of the possible cartons with a volume of one liter that can be made with whole number dimensions.

## Solutions
Some of the possible cartons, their dimensions, and surface areas are listed in the tables. There are many other possibilities not listed here.

| Carton | Length | Width | Height | Volume |
|---|---|---|---|---|
| 1 | 10 | 10 | 10 | 1000 |
| 2 | 1 | 2 | 500 | 1000 |
| 3 | 2 | 5 | 100 | 1000 |
| 4 | 2 | 10 | 50 | 1000 |
| 5 | 4 | 5 | 50 | 1000 |
| 6 | 4 | 10 | 25 | 1000 |
| 7 | 5 | 8 | 25 | 1000 |
| 8 | 20 | 10 | 5 | 1000 |

### Surface Area

| Carton | Face 1 | Face 2 | Face 3 | Face 4 | Face 5 | Face 6 | Total |
|---|---|---|---|---|---|---|---|
| 1 | 100 | 100 | 100 | 100 | 100 | 100 | 600 |
| 2 | 2 | 2 | 500 | 500 | 1000 | 1000 | 3004 |
| 3 | 10 | 10 | 200 | 200 | 500 | 500 | 1420 |
| 4 | 20 | 20 | 100 | 100 | 500 | 500 | 1240 |
| 5 | 20 | 20 | 200 | 200 | 250 | 250 | 940 |
| 6 | 40 | 40 | 100 | 100 | 250 | 250 | 780 |
| 7 | 40 | 40 | 200 | 200 | 125 | 125 | 730 |
| 8 | 200 | 200 | 100 | 100 | 50 | 50 | 700 |

\* Reprinted with permission from *Principles and Standards for School Mathematics*, 2000 by the National Council of Teachers of Mathematics. All rights reserved.

# Looking for a Liter

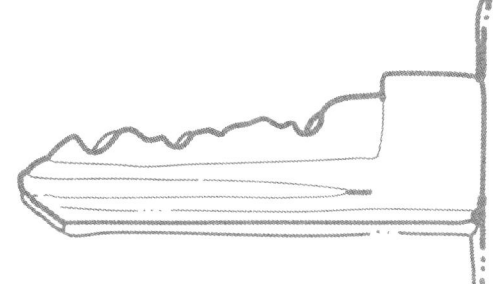

### Key Question

What are the dimensions of some cartons that would hold a liter?

## Learning Goals

### Students will:

- explore volume by finding the dimensions of several cartons that would hold one liter, and

- determine which is the most efficient shape by comparing the surface areas of the different cartons.

# Looking for a Liter

The standard unit of liquid measurement in the metric system is the liter. In many countries, liquids such as milk and juice are sold in liter cartons. Since one liter is equivalent to 1000 milliliters, and a milliliter is equivalent to a cubic centimeter, there are 1000 cubic centimeters in a liter. Therefore, a carton that is 10 cm tall, 10 cm wide, and 10 cm deep would hold one liter of liquid. Your challenge in this activity is to find the dimensions of at least five other cartons that would hold one liter. Record your work in the space below.

1. Which of the dimensions do you think would make the most efficient carton? Why?

2. How would you show that this carton is the most efficient?

# Looking for a Liter

The standard unit of liquid measurement in the metric system is the liter. In many countries, liquids such as milk and juice are sold in liter cartons. Since one liter is equivalent to 1000 milliliters, and a milliliter is equivalent to a cubic centimeter, there are 1000 cubic centimeters in a liter. Therefore, a carton that is 10 cm tall, 10 cm wide, and 10 cm deep would hold one liter of liquid.

Your challenge in this activity is to find the dimensions of at least five other cartons that would hold one liter. Record each carton in the table below. All dimensions are in centimeters. Volume is in cubic centimeters.

| Carton | Length | Width | Height | Volume |
|---|---|---|---|---|
| 1 | 10 | 10 | 10 | 1000 |
| 2 | | | | |
| 3 | | | | |
| 4 | | | | |
| 5 | | | | |
| 6 | | | | |
| 7 | | | | |
| 8 | | | | |

1. Which of the dimensions above do you think would make the most efficient carton? Why?

2. How would you show that this carton is the best?

# Looking for a Liter

To determine the surface area of a carton, you must add the surface areas of each individual face. Fill in the table below to help you determine the total surface area of each of the cartons you found in the first section. The first one has been done for you as an example. Use the following information about the faces to fill in the values:

Face 1 = Length x Width  
Face 2 = Length x Width  
Face 3 = Length x Height  

Face 4 = Length x Height  
Face 5 = Width x Height  
Face 6 = Width x Height  

## Surface Area

| Carton | Face 1 | Face 2 | Face 3 | Face 4 | Face 5 | Face 6 | Total |
|---|---|---|---|---|---|---|---|
| 1 | 100 | 100 | 100 | 100 | 100 | 100 | 600 |
| 2 | | | | | | | |
| 3 | | | | | | | |
| 4 | | | | | | | |
| 5 | | | | | | | |
| 6 | | | | | | | |
| 7 | | | | | | | |
| 8 | | | | | | | |

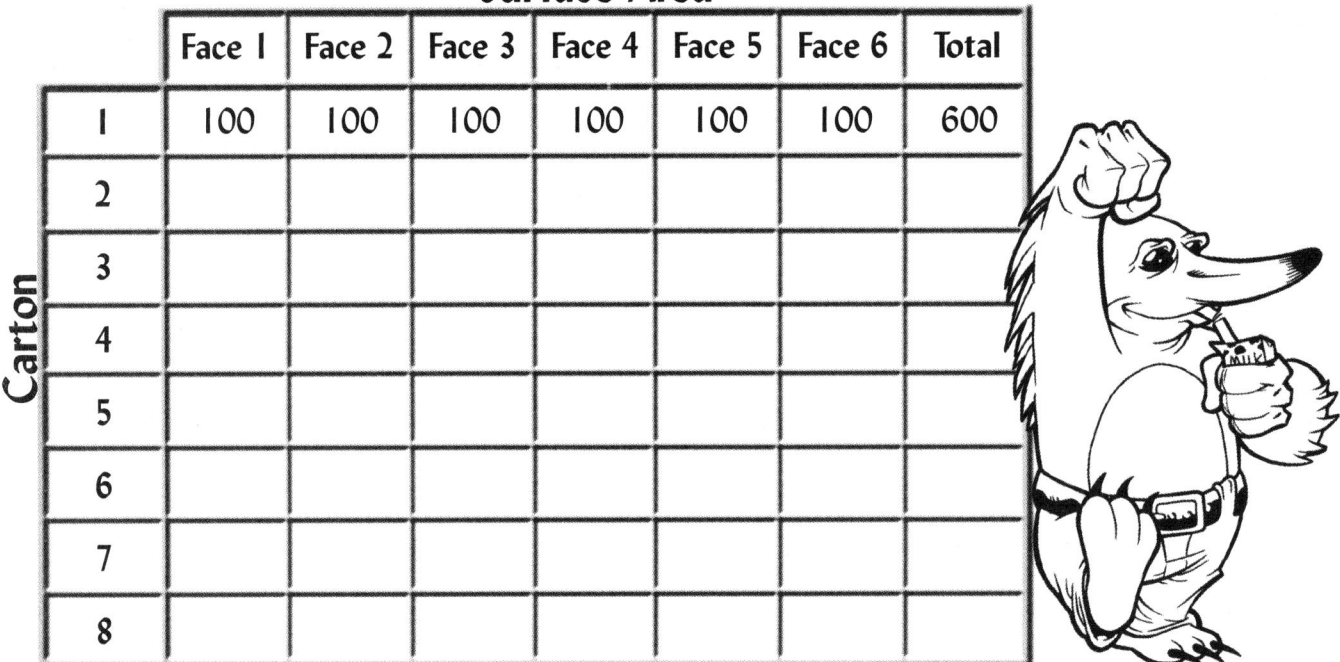

1. Which carton is the most efficient? Why?

2. Is this the same as what you predicted on the first student page? Why or why not?

3. What does this tell you about the cartons you see and use on a daily basis?

JUST FOR THE FUN OF IT! BOOK TWO © 2010 AIMS Education Foundation

# Connecting Learning

1. What are some of the dimensions you were able to find that would hold one liter?

2. Which of these cartons would be the most efficient?

3. How is surface area related to the efficiency of the carton?

4. Why does the 10 x 10 x 10 carton have the smallest surface area?

5. What does this knowledge about surface area tell you about the various cartons you see and use on a daily basis?

# Piecing Together a Paradox

## Topic
Area, mathematical paradoxes

## Key Question
How can you explain the apparent difference in area between shapes that are all made using different configurations of the same four pieces?

## Learning Goals
Students will:
- explore a well-known mathematical paradox,
- attempt to explain it, and
- practice their skills at finding the area of different shapes.

## Guiding Documents
*Project 2061 Benchmarks*
- *Keep record of their investigations and observations and not change the records later.*
- *Length can be thought of as unit lengths joined together, area as a collection of unit squares, and volume as a set of unit cubes.*
- *Offer reasons for their findings and consider reasons suggested by others.*

*NCTM Standards 2000\**
- *Investigate, describe, and reason about the results of subdividing, combining, and transforming shapes*
- *Make and test conjectures about geometric properties and relationships and develop logical arguments to justify conclusions*
- *Use geometric models to solve problems in other areas of mathematics, such as number and measurement*
- *Communicate their mathematical thinking coherently and clearly to peers, teachers, and others*
- *Analyze and evaluate the mathematical thinking and strategies of others*

## Math
Measurement
  area
Geometry and spatial sense
Paradoxes
Problem solving

## Integrated Processes
Observing
Hypothesizing
Collecting and recording data
Comparing and contrasting
Interpreting data

## Problem-Solving Strategies
Use logical thinking
Organize the information

## Materials
Scissors
Student pages
Graph paper, optional
Colored pencils, optional

## Background Information
This activity is a modification of a puzzle that is well known in recreational mathematical circles. The original puzzle is one of those jewels that has intrigued people for more than a hundred years. Lewis Carroll considered it one of his favorite puzzles. Sam Loyd, the great American puzzle creator, also enjoyed it and called it his "dissected checkerboard problem."

The historic puzzle consists of an eight by eight square divided into four pieces. The pieces, when rearranged, appear to form a five by thirteen rectangle. This produces an amazing paradox, since the original square has an area of 64 square units while the rectangle, constructed from the same four pieces, has an apparent area of 65 square units. *Piecing Together a Paradox* expands this original problem and adds to it the element of exploring the areas of various regular and irregular shapes that can be formed using the original four pieces, including one irregular shape with an apparent area of 63 square units.

## Management
1. You may wish to spread this activity over two days, with students finding as many shapes as they can on the first day and calculating the areas of the shapes on the second day.
2. To successfully complete this activity, students will need to carefully cut out the shapes on the first student page. Make sure that they are as precise as possible when they cut, as this will make it easier for them to see the reason for the paradox.

3. You may wish to have your students use colored pencils when they are recording their solutions so that they can distinguish between the different pieces.
4. This activity can be done a few different ways, depending on the ability level of your students. For most elementary students, the first five students pages, which focus on regular polygons, are appropriate. For more advanced students, you can use the last three student pages to introduce them to the Cartesian method for calculating area. This will allow them to find the area of irregular shapes.
5. Unless you plan to use the Cartesian method with your students, you will want to limit the shapes that they calculate the areas of to regular polygons. This is because it is very difficult to find the area of irregular polygons using other methods such as counting squares.
6. If you are using the Cartesian method, you can either have your students use graph paper, or make copies of the mini-graphs page for students to record their shapes.
7. During the discussion time, it is critical that students are able to voice their theories about why the paradox occurs. Hopefully some of your students will discover the actual reason for the paradox and be able to explain it. If not, the solution page can be displayed using a projection device and used to illustrate the difference in the angles of the diagonals that creates the apparent difference in area. This can also be done by students themselves on graph paper.

**Procedure**

*Non-Cartesian Method*
1. Distribute the first two student pages and scissors. Go over the instructions, and make sure that students are very precise when cutting out the shapes. *Carefully cut out the four shapes on your paper. Put them together to make as many different shapes as you can. Make a record of your shapes on the grid paper.*
2. Have students work in groups to come up with as many different shapes as they can using the four pieces. Encourage students to find as many regular shapes as they can, since it is difficult to find the areas of irregular shapes.
3. When groups have found four or more shapes each, hand out the third student page and have students record the areas of the rectangular shapes they created. They should have been able to find a square, a rectangle, and one irregular shape that looks like two squares connected by a long rectangle. If necessary, show students the outline of the irregular shape and have them try to discover how to make it.
4. Allow time for groups to determine the apparent areas of the three rectangular shapes and begin to explore some possible reasons for the paradox.
5. Distribute the fourth student page and have students use the area formulas to determine the (apparent) areas of their regular polygons.
6. When all groups have recorded their shapes' areas, distribute the page of questions and allow them to record their ideas about why the paradox occurs.
7. Be sure each group has had time to come up with an explanation of the paradox before closing with a time of class discussion where students share their discoveries and theories.

*Cartesian Method*
1. Repeat the first five steps of the *Non-Cartesian Method*.
2. Distribute the final three student pages and guide students through the Cartesian method of finding the area, helping them with the examples if necessary.
3. When all groups have recorded their shapes' areas, distribute the page of questions and allow them to record their ideas about why the paradox occurs.
4. Be sure each group has had time to come up with an explanation of the paradox before closing with a time of class discussion where students share their discoveries and theories.

**Connecting Learning**
1. What regular shapes were you able to create using the four pieces? [Square, triangle, rectangle, parallelogram, trapezoid]
2. What areas did you come up with for the various shapes? [63, 64, or 65 square units, depending on the shape.]
3. Which shape appears to have an area of 63 square units? What do you notice about this shape?
4. Which shapes have areas of 64 square units? [square, trapezoid, one parallelogram] What do you notice about these shapes?
5. Which shapes appear to have areas of 65 square units? [triangles, two parallelograms, rectangle] What do you notice about these shapes?
6. How is it possible for the area to change when the pieces you are using stay the same? [It is not possible. The edges of the shapes that have areas other than 64 square units do not form straight lines, accounting for the one square unit difference.]
7. How can you show that this is true? (See *Solutions*.)

### Extensions
1. Have students experiment with cutting a regular polygon into other shapes that will create a similar paradox.
2. Challenge students to show the extra unit square wherever it exists in a shape with an apparent area of 65 square units.

### Solutions
The following diagrams show several of the polygons students should discover and their areas (or apparent areas).

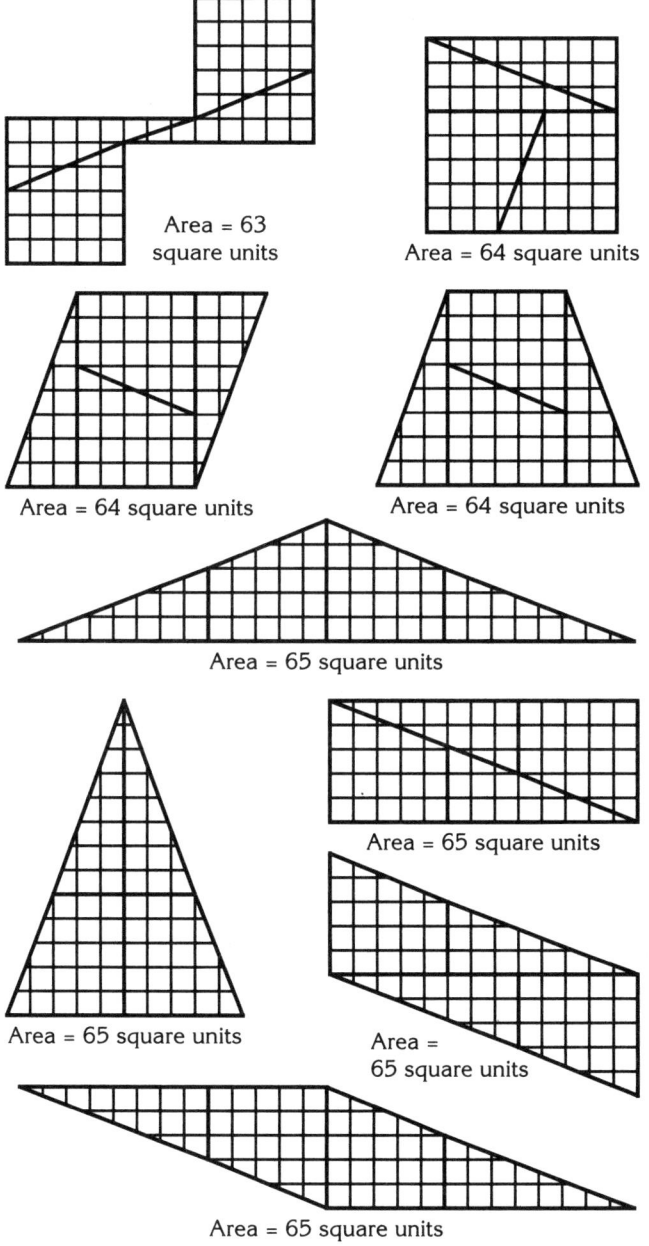

The paradox of this problem has to do with the angles of the lines that make up the shapes. While the triangle and quadrilateral pieces fit together along their common side of three, the angle of their diagonals is just slightly different. It is this difference that accounts for the discrepancies in area between the shapes. As you can see in the diagram here, when a line is drawn from the top vertex to bottom left vertex along the diagonal, there is a small gap between what should be the edge and what actually is the edge given the two shapes.

The diagrams presented on the following page are for the regular polygons with apparent areas of 63 or 65 square units that can be made using the four shapes given. Where appropriate, the actual diagonal has been drawn in. This page can be displayed using a projection device and used during the class discussion time to help students see the paradox. Some of the diagrams make the discrepancy easier to see than others. Especially for the parallelograms, you may want to have students draw the actual and theoretical diagonals on graph paper to see the difference. The answers to student page seven are recorded below.

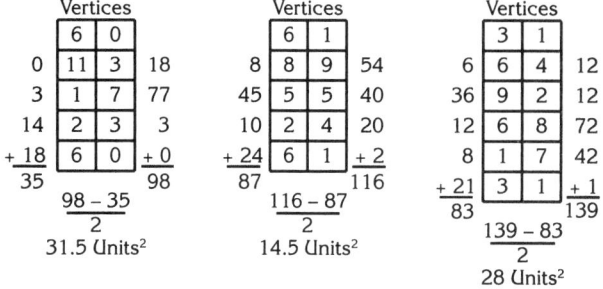

* Reprinted with permission from *Principles and Standards for School Mathematics*, 2000 by the National Council of Teachers of Mathematics. All rights reserved.

# Piecing Together a Paradox

NO...A PARADOX

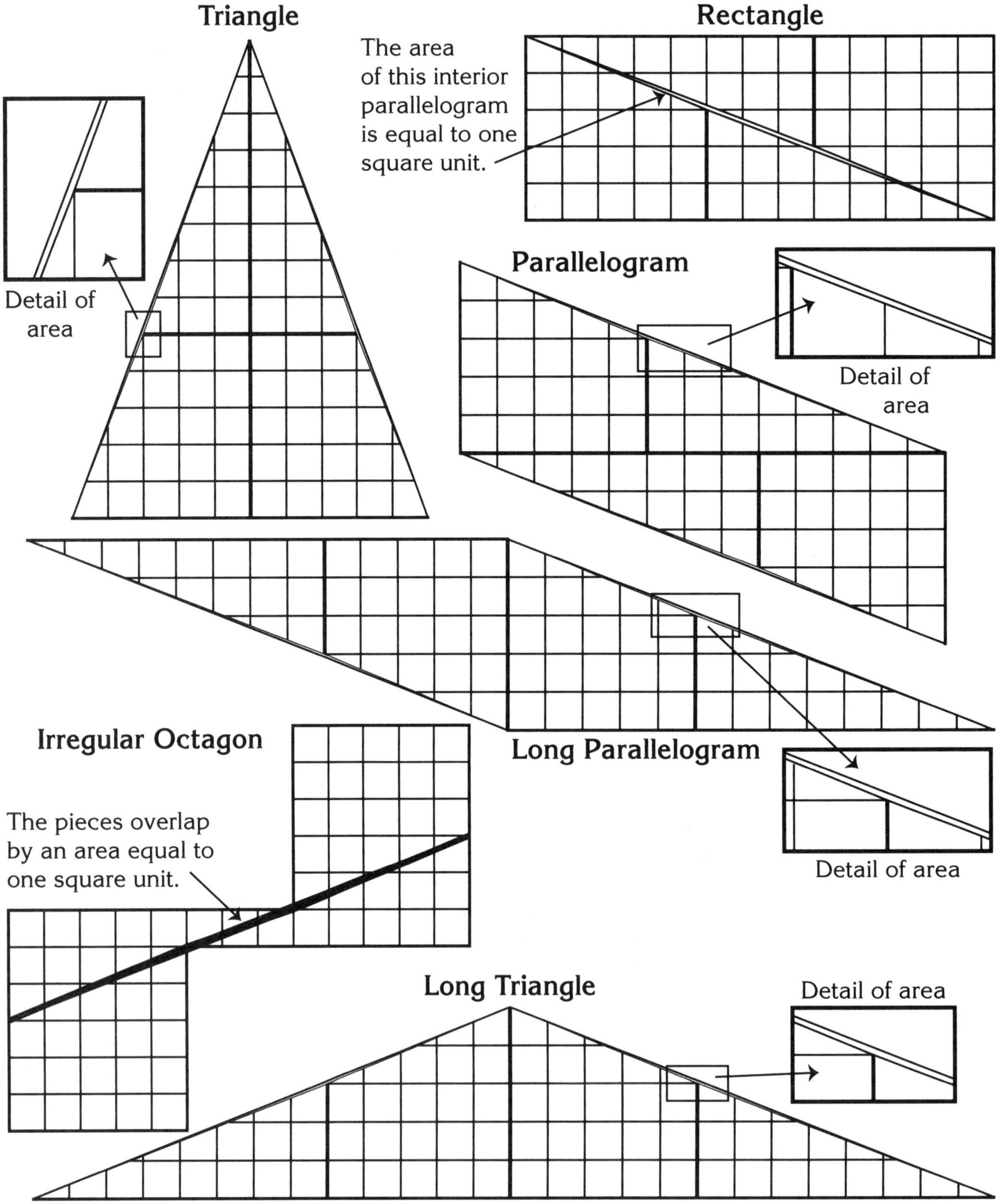

### Triangle

Detail of area

### Rectangle

The area of this interior parallelogram is equal to one square unit.

### Parallelogram

Detail of area

### Long Parallelogram

Detail of area

### Irregular Octagon

The pieces overlap by an area equal to one square unit.

### Long Triangle

Detail of area

JUST FOR THE FUN OF IT! BOOK TWO © 2010 AIMS Education Foundation

## Key Question

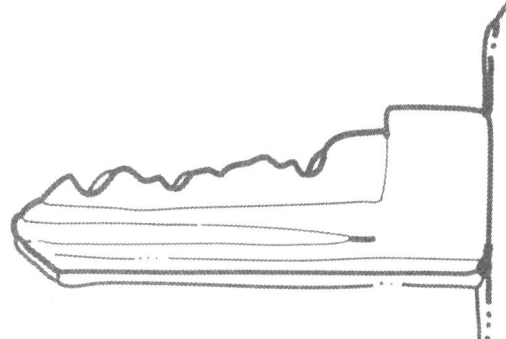

How can you explain the apparent difference in area between shapes that are all made using different configurations of the same four pieces?

## Learning Goals

**Students will:**

- explore a well-known mathematical paradox,

- attempt to explain it, and

- practice their skills at finding the area of different shapes.

# PIECING TOGETHER A PARADOX

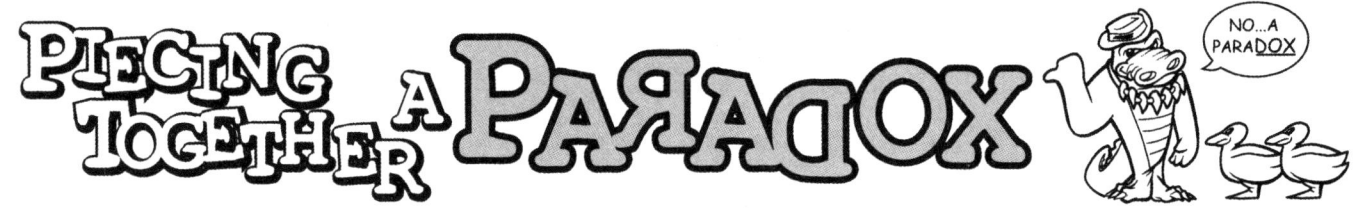

Carefully cut out the four pieces below.
Put them together to make as many different shapes as you can.
Make a record of your shapes in the grid on the next page.

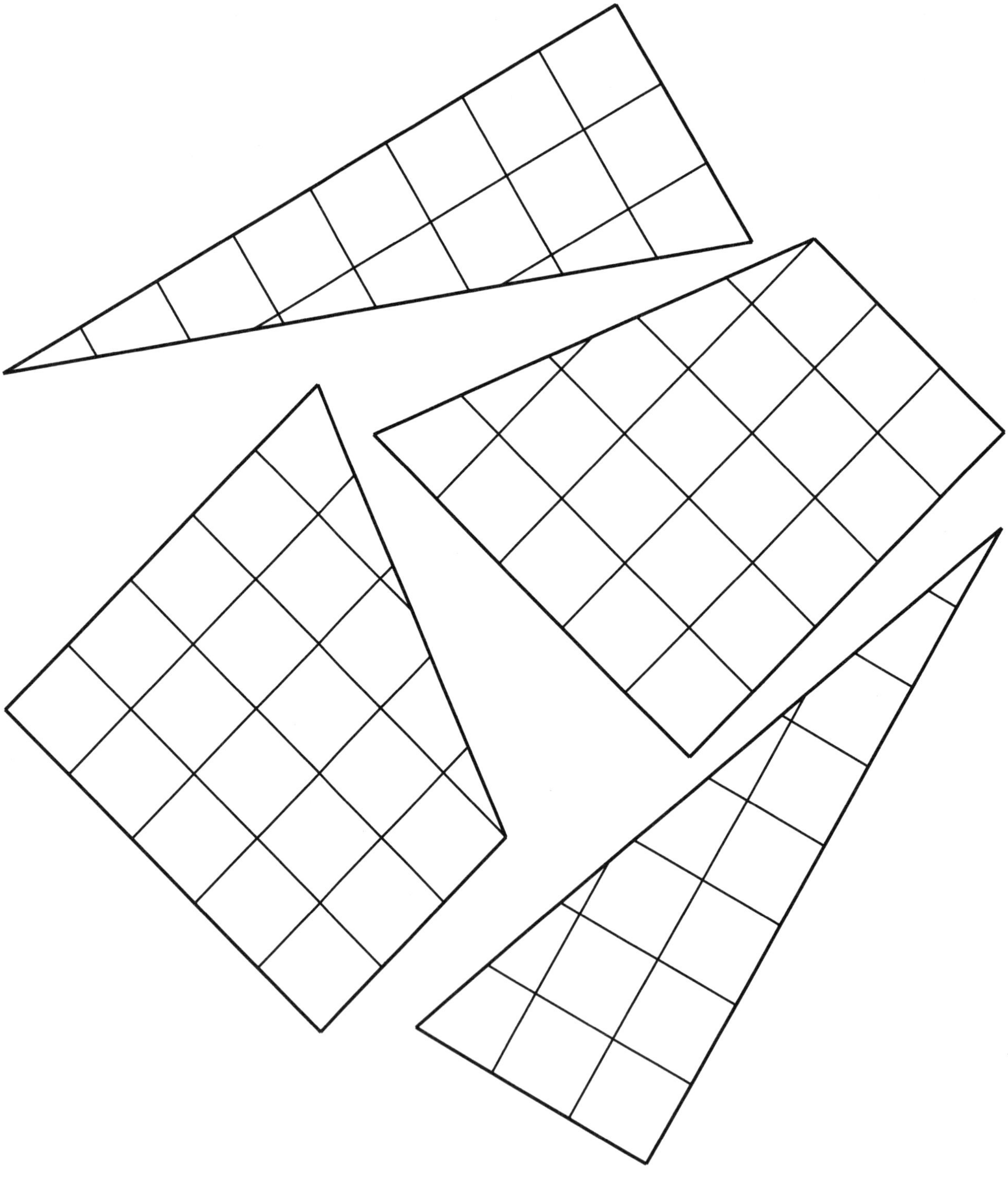

# Piecing Together a Paradox

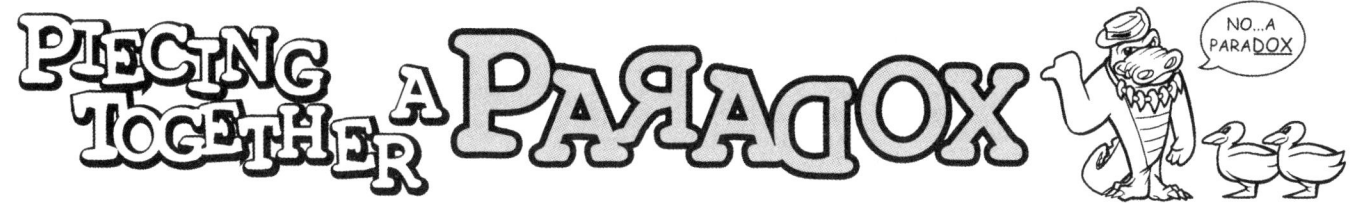

Use the grid below to record the shapes you discover.

Draw all of the rectangular shapes you found in the grid below. You should have three—one square, one rectangle, and one that looks like two squares connected by a long rectangle.

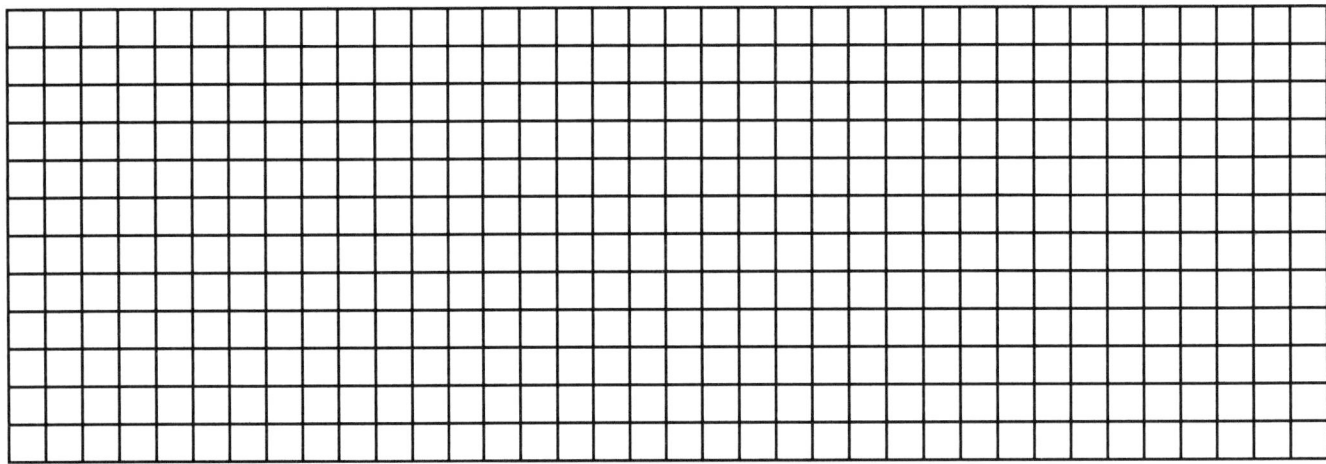

Use the area formula (length x width) or count the squares to find the area of each shape. Record your findings in the table.

| Shape | Area |
| --- | --- |
|  | square units |
|  | square units |
|  | square units |

What do you notice?

How can you explain this?

JUST FOR THE FUN OF IT! BOOK TWO © 2010 AIMS Education Foundation

Look at the non-rectangular shapes you found. Find the area of each one using these formulas.

### Area Formulas for Regular Polygons

| Triangle | $\frac{1}{2}$ (base x height) | |
|---|---|---|
| Parallelogram | base x height | |
| Trapezoid | $\frac{1}{2}(b_1 + b_2)$ x height | |

Record your answers here.

| Shape | Area |
|---|---|
|  |  |
|  |  |
|  |  |
|  |  |
|  |  |
|  |  |
|  |  |
|  |  |

Answer these questions after you have found the areas of all your shapes.

1. What areas do the shapes you found appear to have?

2. Which shape(s) have an area of 63 square units? What do you notice about these shapes?

3. Which shape(s) have an area of 64 square units? What do you notice about these shapes?

4. Which shape(s) have an area of 65 square units? What do you notice about these shapes?

5. Is it possible for these shapes to actually have different areas? Why or why not?

6. How do you explain what is happening?

# Piecing Together a Paradox
## Cartesian Method

Finding the area of irregular polygons can be a simple task when it is done right. With irregular polygons, an area formula will not work, so another method must be used. This method was developed by the mathematician René Descartes and uses what is called the *Cartesian plane*.

To find the area of an irregular polygon, first draw the shape on an x-y coordinate graph. For example:

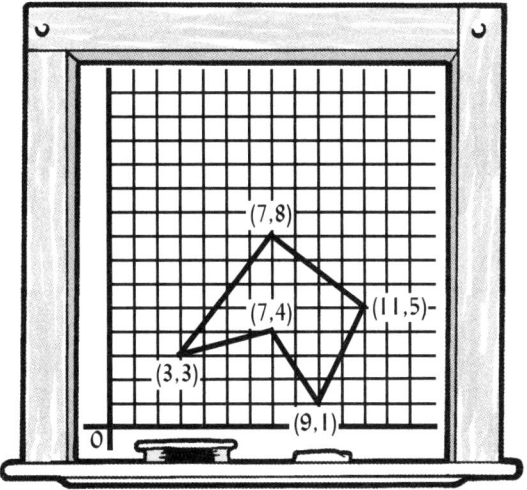

Once you have your shape drawn on a coordinate plane, follow these simple instructions:

1. Beginning with any vertex, list the coordinates of the vertices in order, moving counter-clockwise around the polygon. List the first pair again at the end.

2. Find the diagonal products from left to right.

3. Find the diagonal products from right to left.

4. Sum each column of products.

5. Find their difference and divide by 2.

This is the polygon's area!

| | Verticies | |
|---|---|---|
| | 3 | 3 |
| 21 = | 7 | 4 | = 12
| 36 = | 9 | 1 | = 7
| 11 = | 11 | 5 | = 45
| 35 = | 7 | 8 | = 88
| 24 = | 3 | 3 | = 21
| 127 | | | 173

Area = $\dfrac{173 - 127}{2}$ = 23 square units

Practice using the method you just learned by finding the areas of the irregular polygons below.

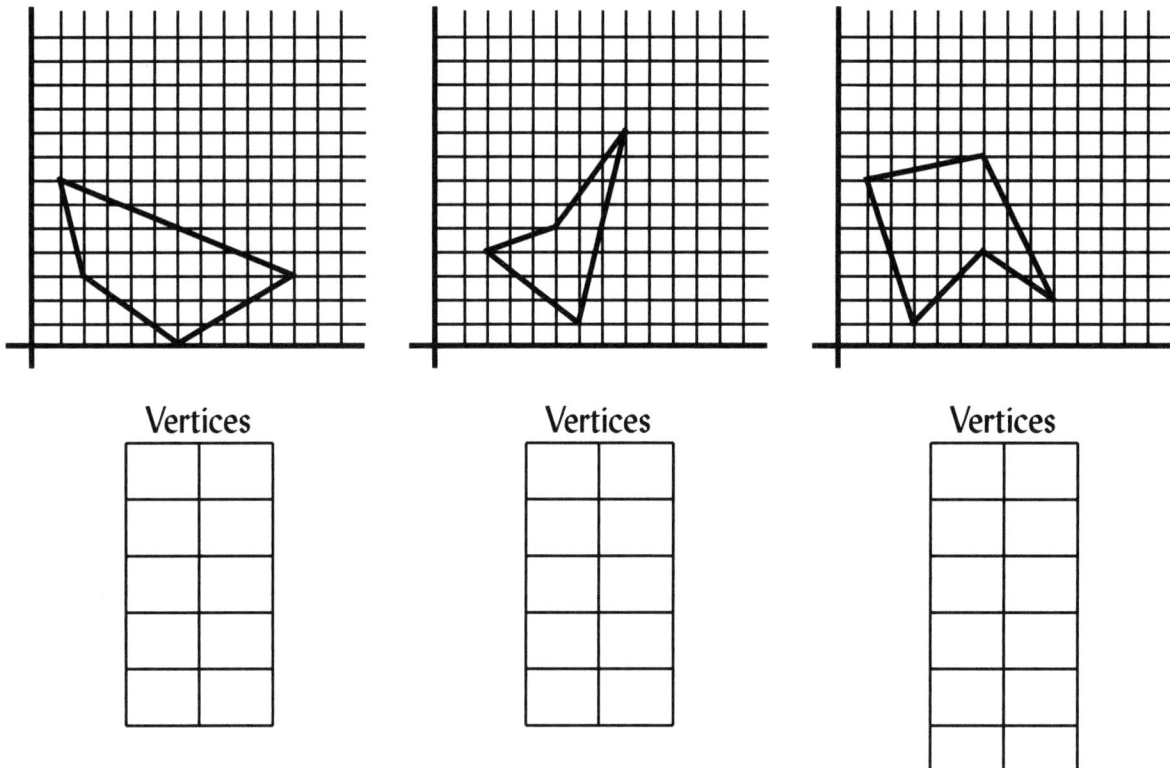

| Vertices | |
|---|---|
|  |  |
|  |  |
|  |  |
|  |  |
|  |  |

| Vertices | |
|---|---|
|  |  |
|  |  |
|  |  |
|  |  |
|  |  |

| Vertices | |
|---|---|
|  |  |
|  |  |
|  |  |
|  |  |
|  |  |

Use the space below to show your work.

JUST FOR THE FUN OF IT! BOOK TWO

# Piecing Together a Paradox
## Cartesian Method

Use the grids below to draw in any irregular shapes that you find. Then use the Cartesian method to determine the area of each shape. Record the areas below each shape.

## Connecting Learning

1. What regular shapes were you able to create using the four pieces?

2. What areas did you come up with for the various shapes?

3. Which shape appears to have an area of 63 square units? What do you notice about this shape?

4. Which shapes have areas of 64 square units? What do you notice about these shapes?

5. Which shapes appear to have areas of 65 square units? What do you notice about these shapes?

6. How is it possible for the area to change when the pieces you are using stay the same?

7. How can you show that this is true?

# CLOCK PALINDROMES

**Topic**
Palindromes

**Key Question**
How many palindromes occur on a digital clock from noon to midnight?

**Learning Goal**
Students will explore palindromes as they record each time that a digital clock displays a palindrome between noon and midnight.

**Guiding Document**
*NCTM Standards 2000**
- *Build new mathematical knowledge through problem solving*
- *Solve problems that arise in mathematics and in other contexts*

**Math**
Palindromes
Math patterns
Problem solving

**Integrated Processes**
Observing
Collecting and recording data

**Problem-Solving Strategy**
Organize the information

**Materials**
Student page

**Background Information**
   This activity explores the palindromes that appear on digital clocks. Palindromes are words, phrases, or numbers that are the same when read from left to right or from right to left. Some examples of palindromic words are *mom, noon, toot,* and *radar.* An example of a palindromic phrase is "Able was I ere I saw Elba." An example of a palindromic number is 1991, the last year in the twentieth century to be a palindrome.
   Over the years, many people have had a fascination with palindromes (some have even formed palindromic societies). Douglas Hofstadter mirrors this fascination in a chapter from his Pulitzer Prize-winning book, *Goedel, Escher, and Bach: An Eternal Golden Braid*. This chapter, entitled *Crab Canon*, begins with a print of the same title by M. C. Escher, the Dutch graphic artist. Escher's *Crab Canon* is a tessellation (a tiling of the plane) that, at first glance, depicts white crabs on a black background. However, on closer inspection, one sees that the black background, which seemed to be just negative space at first, also depicts crabs. When viewed with this focus, one now sees black crabs on a white background. Thus, Escher's print is a sort of visual palindrome. After studying the Escher print at the beginning of the chapter, one reads Hofstadter's *Crab Canon*, a short story that is palindromic in nature and uses characters from Aesop's fables (Achilles and the Tortoise) with the addition of the Crab. The story is a dialogue between Achilles and the Tortoise with a monologue from the Crab sandwiched in the middle. This palindromic dialog can be read from beginning to end or from end to beginning and makes sense both ways. While reading Hofstadter's *Crab Canon*, one begins to appreciate the literary genius that won him the Pulitzer Prize. The chapter ends with a copy of the music score titled *Crab Canon* by Johann Sebastian Bach. When examining this score, even non-musicians can see that it, too, was written as a palindrome (it can be played backwards or forwards and will sound the same either way). In this fashion, Hofstadter shows the reader three variations of a palindromic theme. However, the chapter contains one more element, an intellectual *coup de grace*, that shows the relevance of all this fun, but seemingly petty, palindromic play. This element is an illustration and its accompanying caption tucked away in the middle of the chapter. The illustration depicts the double helix of a crab's DNA. The caption notes that if the two strands of the double helix are unraveled and laid side by side they are mirror images of each other and form a genetic palindrome! Thus, Hofstadter shows us in a powerful way how palindromes are an integral part of our natural world. (If you have not read this book, it is worth checking out from the library for this chapter alone.) While your students may not be able to understand all the intricacies of palindromes (a la Hofstadter), this activity may spur them on to studying palindromes in more depth.

## Management
1. This activity provides a very basic introduction to palindromes. For a more in-depth study, follow this activity with the other palindrome activities found in this volume.
2. *Clock Palindromes* does not have a structured activity page. Because the actual task in this activity is fairly simple, the emphasis is on students developing their own way to discover all of the solutions. Sharing these methods should be the focus of the class discussion time at the end of the activity.
3. If your students are not familiar with palindromes, a brief introduction will be necessary before they can successfully complete the activity.

## Procedure
1. Hand out the student page and go over the instructions, making sure that all students understand what a palindrome is. *Find all the possible number palindromes that appear on a digital clock from noon to midnight.*
2. Have students work together in groups or independently to discover all of the palindromes.
3. Close with a time of class discussion where students share their solutions, the method that they used to arrive at those solutions, and any patterns they noticed while doing the problem.

## Connecting Learning
1. How many palindromes did you find? [There are 57.]
2. What patterns did you notice in your solutions?
3. What method did you use to come up with the answers?

## Extensions
1. Have students find the number of palindromes that would occur on a 24-hour clock such as the ones the military uses.
2. Challenge students to find the number of clock palindromes that would occur in a week or a month.

## Solutions
There are 57 clock palindromes that occur between noon and midnight. Each hour from one to nine has six palindromes, while the hours 10, 11, and 12 have only one each. On a 24-hour clock, there are 64 palindromes. These additional palindromes have been included in italics.

| | | | | | | | | | | |
|---|---|---|---|---|---|---|---|---|---|---|
| 1:01 | 2:02 | 3:03 | 4:04 | 5:05 | 6:06 | 7:07 | 8:08 | 9:09 | 10:01 | *13:31* |
| 1:11 | 2:12 | 3:13 | 4:14 | 5:15 | 6:16 | 7:17 | 8:18 | 9:19 | 11:11 | *14:41* |
| 1:21 | 2:22 | 3:23 | 4:24 | 5:25 | 6:26 | 7:27 | 8:28 | 9:29 | 12:21 | *15:51* |
| 1:31 | 2:32 | 3:33 | 4:34 | 5:35 | 6:36 | 7:37 | 8:38 | 9:39 | | *20:02* |
| 1:41 | 2:42 | 3:43 | 4:44 | 5:45 | 6:46 | 7:47 | 8:48 | 9:49 | | *21:12* |
| 1:51 | 2:52 | 3:53 | 4:54 | 5:55 | 6:56 | 7:57 | 8:58 | 9:59 | | *22:22* |
| | | | | | | | | | | *23:32* |

\* Reprinted with permission from *Principles and Standards for School Mathematics*, 2000 by the National Council of Teachers of Mathematics. All rights reserved.

# CLOCK PALINDROMES

## Key Question

How many palindromes occur on a digital clock from noon to midnight?

## Learning Goal

### Students will:

explore palindromes as they record each time that a digital clock displays a palindrome between noon and midnight.

Palindromes are words, numbers, phrases, etc., that are the same when read from left to right or right to left. For example, *mom* and *dad* are palindromic words, while 343 and 1991 are palindromic numbers. Think of a few other word and number palindromes and write them in the space below.

A digital watch or clock displays number palindromes from time to time during the day. For example, 12:21 and 3:03 are two number palindromes that appear daily. Your challenge in this activity is to find all the possible number palindromes that appear on a digital clock from noon to midnight. Use the space below and the back of this page to work on this problem and to report your findings. If you find any interesting patterns or make any discoveries while working on this activity, be sure to include them in your report. Did you find all the palindromes? How do you know?

## Connecting Learning

1. How many palindromes did you find?

2. What patterns did you notice in your solutions?

3. What method did you use to come up with the answers?

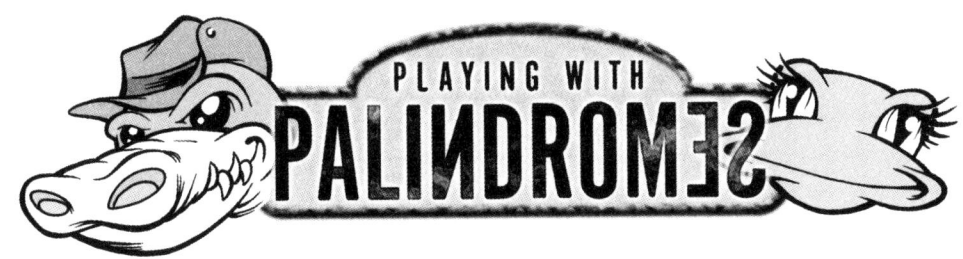

# PLAYING WITH PALINDROMES

**Topic**
Palindromes

**Key Question**
What happens when certain palindromic numbers are doubled and squared?

**Learning Goals**
Students will:
- determine the smallest counting number palindromes having one through four digits;
- double and square these palindromes;
- use the patterns they discovered to determine the smallest seven-digit palindromic number, its double, and its square; and
- repeat this same process with other palindromes.

**Guiding Documents**
*Project 2061 Benchmark*
- *Mathematics is the study of many kinds of patterns, including numbers and shapes and operations on them. Sometimes patterns are studied because they help to explain how the world works or how to solve practical problems, sometimes because they are interesting in themselves.*

*NCTM Standards 2000\**
- *Describe, extend, and make generalizations about geometric and numeric patterns*
- *Build new mathematical knowledge through problem solving*
- *Apply and adapt a variety of appropriate strategies to solve problems*

**Math**
Whole number operations
    addition
    multiplication
Math patterns
Palindromes
Problem solving

**Integrated Processes**
Observing
Inferring
Collecting and recording data
Organizing data
Generalizing

**Problem-Solving Strategies**
Organize the information
Look for patterns

**Materials**
Student pages

**Background Information**
    Palindromes are words, phrases, or numbers that read the same from left to right and right to left. The word palindrome comes from the Greek word *palindromos*, which means running back again. The early Greeks were the first to play with palindromic words and phrases over 2000 years ago, and this fascination has not abated in the intervening years.
    In *Playing with Palindromes*, students look at what happens when certain palindromic numbers are doubled and squared. (For students who are not familiar with squaring, this activity is a good introduction to the concept.)

**Management**
1. This activity is best done in small groups of three to five students.
2. Each student will need his or her own copy of the student pages.

**Procedure**
1. Distribute the first student page and go over the instructions as a class. Be sure everyone understands the challenge.
2. Give students time to complete the first page individually, then have them work in small groups to compare their answers and discuss the patterns they notice.
3. Have groups share their answers and the patterns they discovered with the class.
4. Distribute the second and third student pages and repeat this process.
5. Close with a final time of class discussion and sharing.

**Connecting Learning**

1. What is the smallest one-digit palindromic number? [1] ...the smallest two-digit palindromic number? [11] ...three digit? [101] ...four digit? [1001]
2. What happens when you double and square these numbers? [You get palindromes.]
3. What patterns did your group notice in the first table? [The squared palindromes always start and end with 1 and have a 2 in the middle.]
4. What patterns did you discover in the second part of the activity? (See *Solutions*.)
5. Why doesn't the pattern hold true for the 10-digit palindrome? [because you have to carry a one]
6. What other palindromic patterns did you discover?

**Solutions**

The tables from the first two student pages are shown here.

*Part One*

**Counting Number Palindromes**

|  | Smallest one-digit palindrome | Smallest two-digit palindrome | Smallest three-digit palindrome | Smallest four-digit palindrome |
|---|---|---|---|---|
| Original palindrome | 1 | 11 | 101 | 1001 |
| Original palindrome doubled | 2 | 22 | 202 | 2002 |
| Original palindrome squared | 1 | 121 | 10201 | 1002001 |

*Part Two*

| Palindrome | 1 | 11 | 111 | 1111 |
|---|---|---|---|---|
| Doubled | 2 | 22 | 222 | 2222 |
| Squared | 1 | 121 | 12321 | 1234321 |

| Palindrome | Doubled | Squared |
|---|---|---|
| 11111 | 22222 | 123454321 |
| 111111 | 222222 | 12345654321 |
| 1111111 | 2222222 | 1234567654321 |
| 11111111 | 22222222 | 123456787654321 |
| 111111111 | 222222222 | 12345678987654321 |

Using palindromes consisting entirely of ones, the doubling pattern will continue infinitely, but the squaring pattern only continues up to 111111111 (nine ones) whose square is 12345678987654321. When 10 ones are squared, the pattern no longer holds—the square is 1234567900987654321. This occurs because when adding 10 ones, you have to carry a one, causing a breakdown of the pattern.

\* Reprinted with permission from *Principles and Standards for School Mathematics*, 2000 by the National Council of Teachers of Mathematics. All rights reserved.

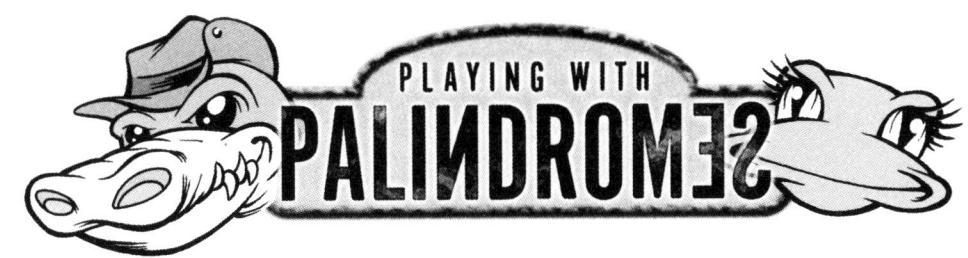

## Key Question

What happens when certain palindromic numbers are doubled and squared?

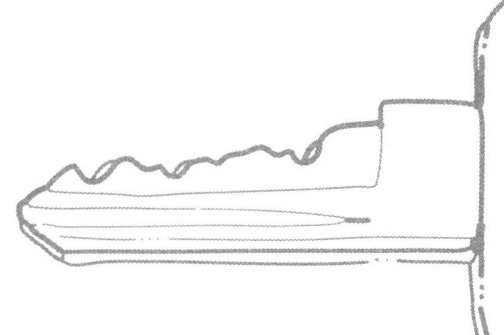

## Learning Goals

### Students will:

- determine the smallest counting number palindromes having one through four digits;
- double and square these palindromes;
- use the patterns they discovered to determine the smallest seven-digit palindromic number, its double, and its square; and
- repeat this same process with other palindromes.

# PLAYING WITH PALINDROMES
## DOUBLING AND SQUARING

A palindromic number is one that is the same when read from left to right and right to left. The year 2002 is an example of a palindromic number. When you double this number, you get 4004, which is also a palindrome. When you square 2002 (multiply it by itself), you get 4008004—another palindrome. Not all palindromic numbers produce palindromes when doubled or squared, but some do. In this activity you will explore some of these numbers.

What is the smallest palindromic counting number? (The counting numbers are the infinite set of numbers that begin with 1, 2, 3, 4, 5, ...) What is the smallest two-digit palindromic counting number? The smallest three-digit palindromic counting number? (Don't let this one trick you.) The smallest four-digit one? List these palindromes in the first row of the chart below. Next, double each one and put the resulting numbers in the second row. Finally, square each of the original palindromes and record the answers in the third row of the chart.

|  | Smallest one-digit palindrome | Smallest two-digit palindrome | Smallest three-digit palindrome | Smallest four-digit palindrome |
|---|---|---|---|---|
| Original palindrome |  |  |  |  |
| Original palindrome doubled |  |  |  |  |
| Original palindrome squared |  |  |  |  |

What patterns do you notice in the above numbers? List as many patterns as you can here, then use them to find the smallest seven-digit palindrome, its double, and its square.

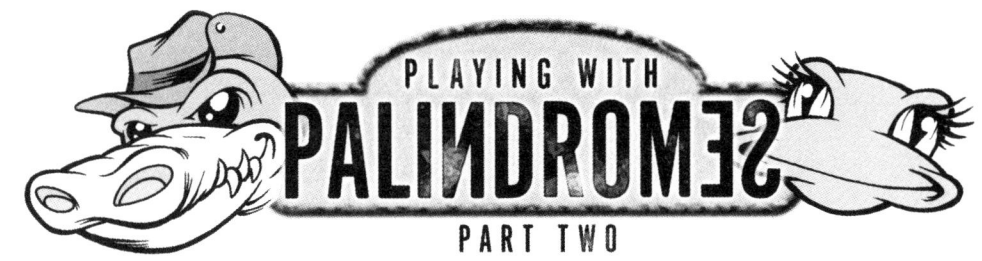

# PLAYING WITH PALINDROMES
## PART TWO

1. Here is another series of palindromes. Find the double and square of each and record it in the table below.

| Palindrome | 1 | 11 | 111 | 1111 |
|---|---|---|---|---|
| Doubled | | | | |
| Squared | | | | |

2. What patterns do you see in the table?




3. Use these patterns to fill in the doubles and squares for the next five numbers in the series.

| Palindrome | Doubled | Squared |
|---|---|---|
| 11111 | | |
| 111111 | | |
| 1111111 | | |
| 11111111 | | |
| 111111111 | | |

4. Predict what will happen to these patterns with the next palindrome in the series—**1111111111**.

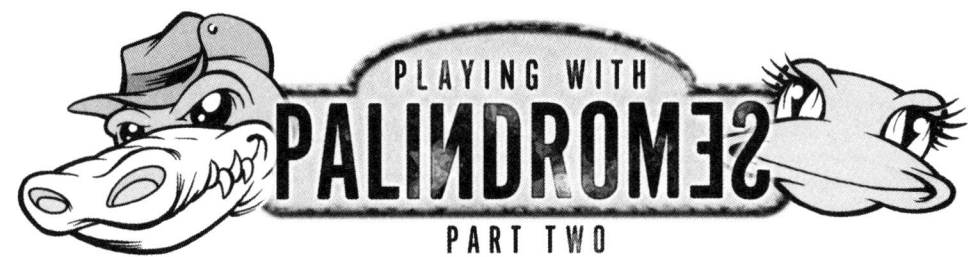

## PART TWO

5. Use the spaces provided to test your predictions.

```
  1 1 1 1 1 1 1 1 1 1
+ 1 1 1 1 1 1 1 1 1 1
```

```
     1 1 1 1 1 1 1 1 1 1
  x  1 1 1 1 1 1 1 1 1 1
```

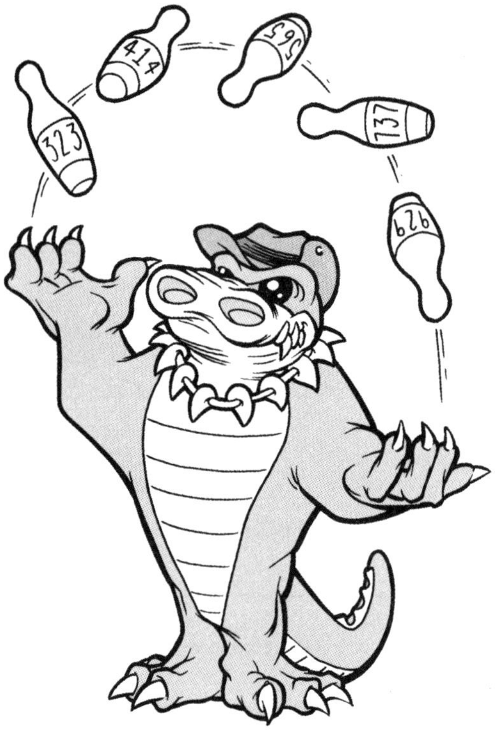

6. Explain why one of the patterns does not hold true for the 10-digit palindrome.

7. Think of another series of palindromic numbers. Play around with these palindromes and see what you discover. Be ready to report your findings to the class.

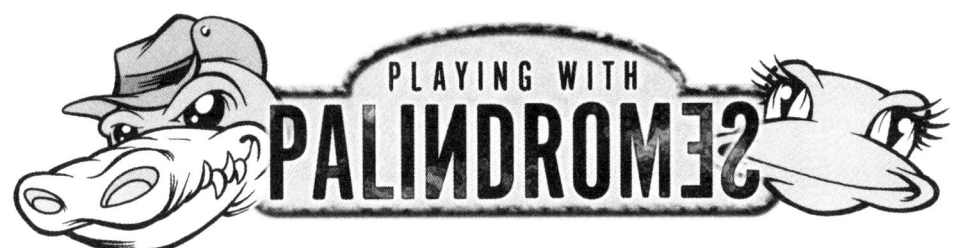

# Connecting Learning

1. What is the smallest one-digit palindromic number? ...the smallest two-digit palindromic number? ...three digit? ...four digit?

2. What happens when you double and square these numbers?

3. What patterns did your group notice in the first table?

4. What patterns did you discover in the second part of the activity?

5. Why doesn't the pattern hold true for the 10-digit palindrome?

6. What other palindromic patterns did you discover?

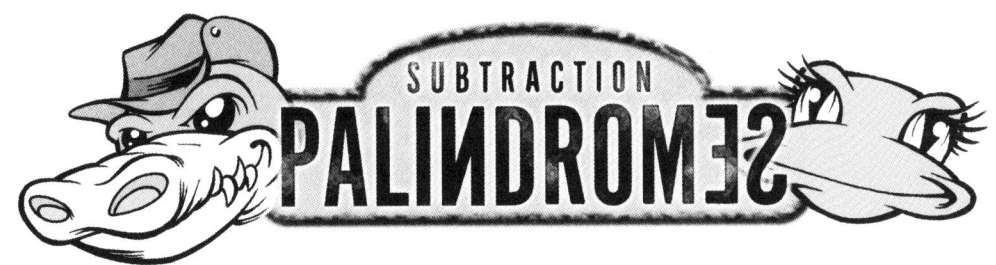

# SUBTRACTION PALINDROMES

**Topic**
Palindromes

**Key Question**
What patterns can you discover in the process of making any two-digit number a palindrome through subtraction?

**Learning Goals**
Students will:
* use a reversal and subtraction process for making any two digit number a palindrome, and
* look for patterns in their solutions.

**Guiding Documents**
*Project 2061 Benchmark*
* *Mathematics is the study of many kinds of patterns, including numbers and shapes and operations on them. Sometimes patterns are studied because they help to explain how the world works or how to solve practical problems, sometimes because they are interesting in themselves.*

*NCTM Standards 2000\**
* *Describe, extend, and make generalizations about geometric and numeric patterns*
* *Build new mathematical knowledge through problem solving*

**Math**
Palindromes
Subtraction
Math patterns
Problem solving

**Integrated Processes**
Observing
Comparing and contrasting

**Problem-Solving Strategies**
Organize the information
Look for patterns

**Materials**
Colored pencils or crayons
Scratch paper
Student pages

**Background Information**
In *Subtraction Palindromes,* students discover what happens when they take a two-digit number, reverse the digits, place the larger of the two numbers on top, and then find the difference. This process always produces either the number nine, which is a palindrome (a number that is the same when read from right to left or left to right), or two digits with a sum of nine (e.g., 76 – 67 = 9; 50 – 05 = 45). In the cases where this process doesn't produce a nine on the first reversal and subtraction, students will repeat it until a nine is produced. In the second example above, the 45 is reduced to a nine in one more step (54 – 45 = 9). Following this process with any two-digit number that is not already a palindrome will produce the palindrome nine in either one, two, three, four, or five steps. In this activity, numbers that are already palindromes (00, 11, 22, etc.) are considered zero-step subtraction palindromes. Students are challenged to find the number of subtraction steps necessary to produce the palindrome nine for all the numbers from 00-99. *Note that in this activity, single-digit numbers are written with a zero in the tens place to help preserve the inherent symmetry.*

**Management**
1. In order for students to discover the patterns in this activity, they need to organize their data in a logical way. If your students are accomplished problem solvers and you want them to approach this activity in an open-ended manner, use only the first student page, which introduces the problem. For those students who need more structure to help them organize the data, the second through fourth student pages are appropriate.
2. The fifth student page has questions to help students pull together their thoughts and discoveries and can be used with both the open-ended and the structured approach.
3. In both the open-ended and the structured formats, students will need scratch paper on which to work out the problems.
4. There are some important discoveries that students should make that will reduce the amount of work they need to do in this activity. For example, when they find that 89 is a one-step subtraction palindrome, they should see that 98 also takes one-step, and that they can record this information without redoing the problem.

JUST FOR THE FUN OF IT! BOOK TWO        © 2010 AIMS Education Foundation

## Procedure

*Open-Ended Format*

1. Distribute the first student page and go over the method students will be using to find the subtraction palindromes. If necessary, do a few more examples as a class to be sure that students clearly understand the process.
2. Give students scratch paper on which to work out the problems and organize their findings. Have them work together in groups to determine the subtraction palindromes for all of the two-digit numbers from 00 to 99.
3. When groups are finished, hand out the final student page and have students answer the questions.
4. If time allows, challenge students to think of extensions to this problem and explore them.
5. Close with a time of class discussion and sharing where you go over the student pages and have students articulate the patterns they discovered in the problem.

*Structured Format*

1. Distribute the first student page and go over the method students will be using to find the subtraction palindromes. If necessary, do a few more examples as a class to be sure that students clearly understand the process.
2. Hand out the second and third student pages and scratch paper and have students work together in small groups to find the subtraction palindromes for all of the two-digit numbers from 00 to 99.
3. When all of the groups have completed both tables, hand out the fourth student page and colored pencils so that students can complete the chart.
4. When groups are finished with the chart, distribute the final student page and have students answer the questions.
5. If time allows, challenge students to think of extensions to this problem and explore them.
6. Close with a time of class discussion and sharing where you go over the student pages and have students articulate the patterns they discovered in the problem.

## Connecting Learning

1. How many zero-step subtraction palindromes are there in the numbers from zero to 99? [10]
2. How many one-step? [18] ...two-step? [18] ...three-step? [18] ...four-step? [18] ...five-step? [18]
3. What do you notice about all of the numbers that are one-step palindromes? [The difference between the two digits is one.]
4. Do you see any similar patterns with numbers that are two-, three-, four-, and five-step palindromes? (See *Solutions*.)
5. What patterns do you see in the colored chart?
6. How do these patterns relate to the other patterns that you have discovered?
7. What extensions did you think of to explore?
8. What were your findings?

## Extensions

1. See *Palindromic Ponderings* for an in-depth study of addition palindromes.
2. If students are able to deal with integers, have them do this activity without placing the larger number on top before subtracting. This will result in one of four palindromic numbers: -99, -9, 0, and 9.
3. Try the original process with three-digit numbers. What palindrome(s) would you predict as results? Were you correct?

## Solutions

Although the patterns in subtraction palindromes are much more subtle than those in addition palindromes, they are interesting none the less. Several of the patterns and mathematical discoveries that your students should uncover are discussed below.

- Nine is the only palindrome produced when subtracting two-digit numbers using the given process.
- The differences (other than nine) produced when reversing and subtracting are all two-digit numbers, and the sum of those two digits is always nine.
- Some numbers take one reversal and subtraction to produce a palindrome. These are called one-step subtraction palindromes. Numbers that take two reversals and subtractions to produce a palindrome are called two-step subtraction palindromes. Those that take three reversals are three-step, and so on. There are 10 zero-step palindromes, and 18 each of the one- through five-step palindromes.
- The difference between the digits in the numbers that are one-step subtraction palindromes is one. For example, 12, 21, 23, 32, 34, and 43 are all one-step subtraction palindromes.
- The difference between the digits in two-step subtraction palindromes is either five or six. For example, 50 and 05 (difference of five), and 71 and 17 (difference of six) are two-step subtraction palindromes.
- With three-step palindromes, the difference between the digits is either three or eight.
- Four-step palindromes have differences of four or seven between their digits.
- Five-step palindromes have differences of two or nine between their digits.

\* Reprinted with permission from *Principles and Standards for School Mathematics*, 2000 by the National Council of Teachers of Mathematics. All rights reserved.

# SUBTRACTION PALINDROMES

## Key Question

What patterns can you discover in the process of making any two-digit number a palindrome through subtraction?

## Learning Goals

- use a reversal and subtraction process for making any two digit number a palindrome, and

- look for patterns in their solutions.

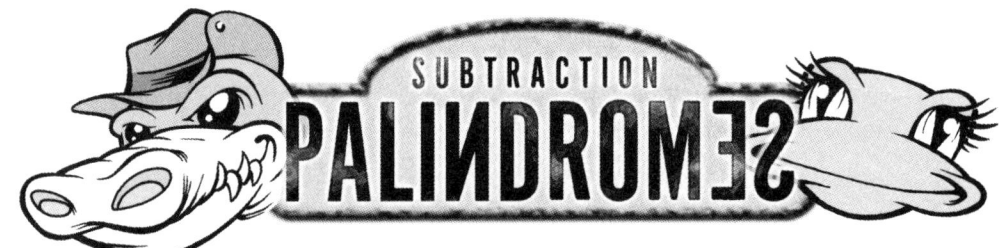

# SUBTRACTION PALINDROMES

Palindromes are numbers that are the same when read from left to right or right to left. Numbers like 11, 747, and 2002 are all palindromic numbers.

Any two-digit number that is not already a palindrome can be made into the palindrome nine using the special method of subtracting described below.

Start with any two-digit number. Reverse the order of the digits and place the larger of the two numbers on top. Find the difference between these numbers. If the difference is not a palindrome, repeat this process until a palindrome is formed.

Let's try this process with the numbers 32 and 12.

    32 (starting #)      12 (starting #)      21 (place larger # on top)
− 23 (reverse digits, subtract)      21 (reverse digits)      − 12 (subtract)
     9 (palindrome)                                                    9 (palindrome)

We call the above numbers one-step subtraction palindromes because they can be made into a palindrome by reversing and subtracting once. Not all numbers are one-step subtraction palindromes, however. Some take two, three, four, or even five steps. Let's see how the process works with a three-step palindrome.

    30 (starting #)      72 (larger # on top)      54 (larger # on top)
− 03 (reverse digits, subtract)      − 27 (subtract)      − 45 (subtract)
    27 (not a palindrome)      45 (not a palindrome)      9 (palindrome)
    72 (reverse digits)        54 (reverse digits)

Use this process on the numbers 43, 34, 28, and 82 and show your work below.

Your challenge in this activity is to find how many steps it takes to produce a subtraction palindrome for each two-digit number from 00-99. What do you notice about the four problems that you did above that might save you time when doing this?

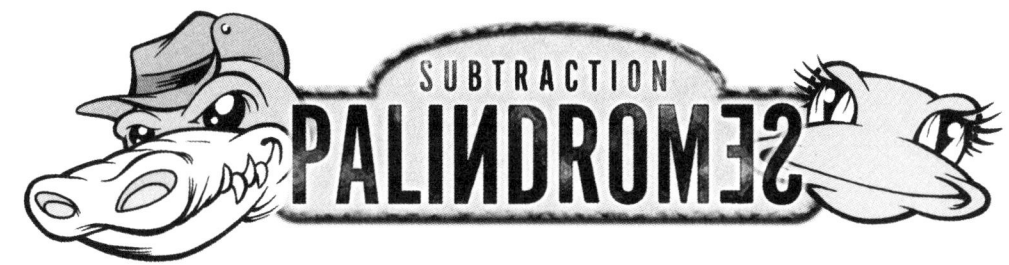

Use the space in the chart below to find the number of subtraction steps it takes to produce a palindrome for the numbers from 80 to 99. Continue in this format on scratch paper for the rest of the numbers from 00 to 70.

| | |
|---|---|
| 80    72<br>− 08  − 27<br>   72 | 90 |
| 81<br>− 18 | 91 |
| 82 | 92 |
| 83 | 93 |
| 84 | 94 |
| 85 | 95 |
| 86 | 96 |
| 87 | 97 |
| 88 already a palindrome (zero-step) | 98 done (see 89) |
| 89 | 99 already a palindrome (zero-step) |

JUST FOR THE FUN OF IT! BOOK TWO

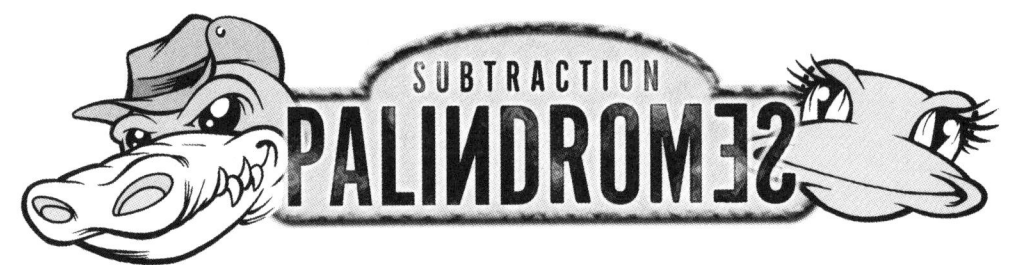

Complete the table below, indicating how many steps it takes each number to be changed into a palindrome using the subtraction method.

| # | Steps | # | Steps | # | Steps | # | Steps |
|---|---|---|---|---|---|---|---|
| 00 | | 25 | | 50 | | 75 | |
| 01 | | 26 | | 51 | | 76 | |
| 02 | | 27 | | 52 | | 77 | |
| 03 | | 28 | | 53 | | 78 | |
| 04 | | 29 | | 54 | | 79 | |
| 05 | | 30 | | 55 | | 80 | |
| 06 | | 31 | | 56 | | 81 | |
| 07 | | 32 | | 57 | | 82 | |
| 08 | | 33 | | 58 | | 83 | |
| 09 | | 34 | | 59 | | 84 | |
| 10 | | 35 | | 60 | | 85 | |
| 11 | | 36 | | 61 | | 86 | |
| 12 | | 37 | | 62 | | 87 | |
| 13 | | 38 | | 63 | | 88 | |
| 14 | | 39 | | 64 | | 89 | |
| 15 | | 40 | | 65 | | 90 | |
| 16 | | 41 | | 66 | | 91 | |
| 17 | | 42 | | 67 | | 92 | |
| 18 | | 43 | | 68 | | 93 | |
| 19 | | 44 | | 69 | | 94 | |
| 20 | | 45 | | 70 | | 95 | |
| 21 | | 46 | | 71 | | 96 | |
| 22 | | 47 | | 72 | | 97 | |
| 23 | | 48 | | 73 | | 98 | |
| 24 | | 49 | | 74 | | 99 | |

JUST FOR THE FUN OF IT! BOOK TWO

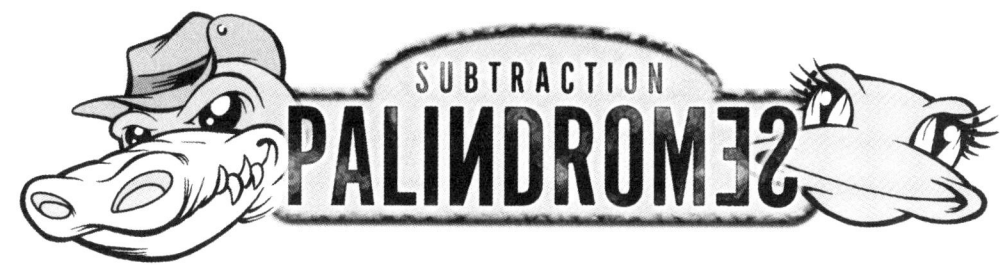

# SUBTRACTION PALINDROMES

Use the information from the table on the previous page to color in the chart below. Choose a color for each number of steps and use it to shade the squares containing the numbers that use that many steps.

## KEY

- [ ] zero steps
- [ ] one step
- [ ] two steps
- [ ] three steps
- [ ] four steps
- [ ] five steps

| 00 | 01 | 02 | 03 | 04 | 05 | 06 | 07 | 08 | 09 |
| 10 | 11 | 12 | 13 | 14 | 15 | 16 | 17 | 18 | 19 |
| 20 | 21 | 22 | 23 | 24 | 25 | 26 | 27 | 28 | 29 |
| 30 | 31 | 32 | 33 | 34 | 35 | 36 | 37 | 38 | 39 |
| 40 | 41 | 42 | 43 | 44 | 45 | 46 | 47 | 48 | 49 |
| 50 | 51 | 52 | 53 | 54 | 55 | 56 | 57 | 58 | 59 |
| 60 | 61 | 62 | 63 | 64 | 65 | 66 | 67 | 68 | 69 |
| 70 | 71 | 72 | 73 | 74 | 75 | 76 | 77 | 78 | 79 |
| 80 | 81 | 82 | 83 | 84 | 85 | 86 | 87 | 88 | 89 |
| 90 | 91 | 92 | 93 | 94 | 95 | 96 | 97 | 98 | 99 |

JUST FOR THE FUN OF IT! BOOK TWO

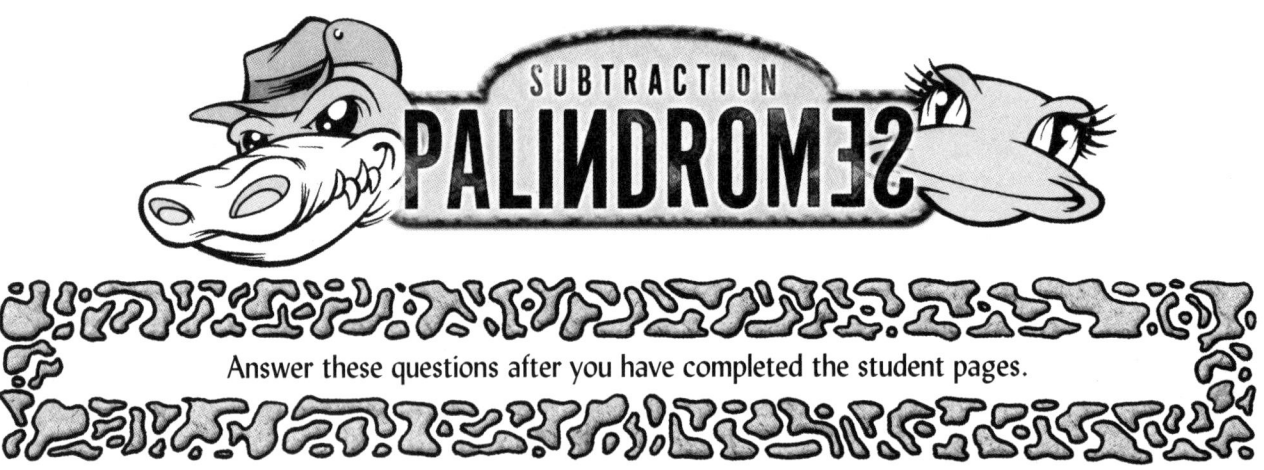

Answer these questions after you have completed the student pages.

1. How many zero-step subtraction palindromes are there in the numbers zero to 99?

2. How many one-step? …two-step? …three-step? …four-step? …five-step?

3. What do you notice about all of the numbers that are one-step palindromes?

4. Do you see any similar patterns with the numbers that are two-step palindromes? …three-step palindromes? …four-step? …five-step?

5. What patterns do you see in the colored chart?

6. How do these patterns relate to the other patterns that you have discovered?

**Challenge**: Think of an extension to this activity. Explore this extension and report your findings.

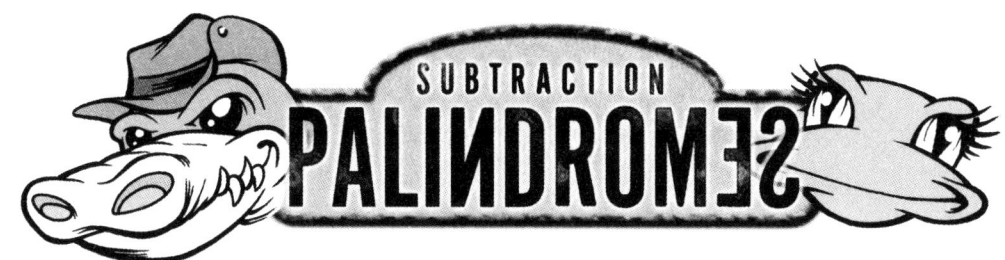

## Connecting Learning

1. How many zero-step subtraction palindromes are there in the numbers from zero to 99?

2. How many one-step? ...two-step? ...three-step? ...four-step? ...five-step?

3. What do you notice about all of the numbers that are one-step palindromes?

4. Do you see any similar patterns with numbers that are two-, three-, four-, and five-step palindromes?

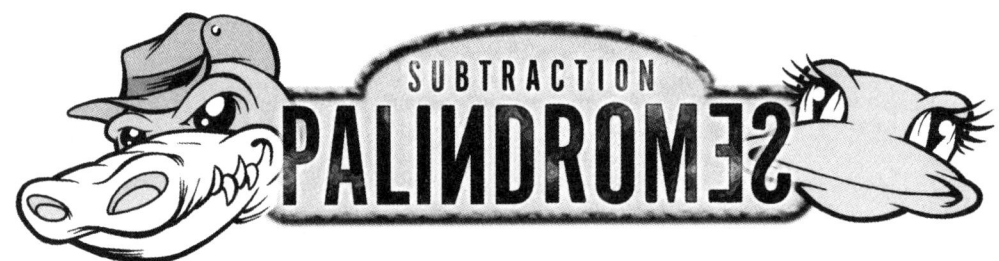

## Connecting Learning

5. What patterns do you see in the colored chart?

6. How do these patterns relate to the other patterns that you have discovered?

7. What extensions did you think of to explore?

8. What were your findings?

# Palindromic Ponderings

**Topic**
Palindromes

**Key Question**
What patterns can you discover in palindromes?

**Learning Goal**
Students will explore some of the fascinating properties and patterns that stem from the *palindrome conjecture*.

**Guiding Documents**
*Project 2061 Benchmark*
- *Mathematics is the study of many kinds of patterns, including numbers and shapes and operations on them. Sometimes patterns are studied because they help to explain how the world works or how to solve practical problems, sometimes because they are interesting in themselves.*

*NCTM Standards 2000\**
- *Describe, extend, and make generalizations about geometric and numeric patterns*
- *Build new mathematical knowledge through problem solving*

**Math**
Whole number operations
Math patterns
Palindromes
Problem solving

**Integrated Processes**
Observing
Inferring
Collecting and recording data
Generalizing

**Problem-Solving Strategies**
Organize the information
Look for patterns

**Materials**
Crayons, markers, or colored pencils
Student pages
Calculators, optional see *(Management 6)*

**Background Information**
In this activity, students will explore some of the fascinating properties and patterns that stem from the *palindrome conjecture*. Martin Gardner talks about this problem in his book, *Aha! Insight*: "There is a famous unsolved number problem called the 'palindrome conjecture.'" (Gardner, 1978, p. 152) This conjecture, according to Gardner, states that any positive integer can be made into a palindrome (in a finite number of steps) by following a simple procedure. In this procedure, the digits of the original number are reversed. The new number formed is then added to the original number. If the sum is a palindrome, the procedure ends; if not, the process is repeated until a palindrome is produced. For example, 39 is not a palindrome but generates a palindrome in two steps:

$$\begin{array}{r} 39 \\ + 93 \\ \hline 132 \\ + 231 \\ \hline 363 \end{array}$$

Gardner states that no one knows for sure if the conjecture is true or not, but mathematicians have found many numbers that have not yet produced palindromes, even after thousands of steps. The smallest of these numbers, 196, has been taken to hundreds of thousands of steps by computers without producing a palindrome. However, no one has yet proven conclusively that it will *never* produce one.

By finding the palindromes created by the numbers 0 to 99, students will discover some patterns that exist and learn to make logical predictions and generalizations about palindromes.

**Management**
1. This activity is rather time consuming, and should not be rushed, so make sure you have adequate time to complete it before beginning.
2. Because of the in-depth nature of this activity, it is recommended that this not be students' first exposure to palindromes. The preceding activities in this volume are good ones to introduce students to palindromes.

JUST FOR THE FUN OF IT! BOOK TWO     159     © 2010 AIMS Education Foundation

3. Student page one provides a description of palindromes as well as the instructions for the activity. It is not necessary to hand out this page to your students, although it may be useful for them to have. If you do not give them a copy of this page, be sure to go over the information it covers as a class before you start the activity. You may want to display the page using a projection device for this purpose.
4. Each student will need two copies of student page two for this activity because there are only 50 spaces on the page and 100 spaces are needed.
5. Students will need seven different colors of crayons, colored pencils, or markers to complete the chart on student page three.
6. Due to the large sums that students will be computing as they add some of the larger numbers, calculators are recommended. This will not only cut down on the time it takes to complete this activity, it can also help eliminate error as students compute the six- and 24-step palindromes.
7. Have students work together in groups. This will keep them from being overwhelmed by the magnitude of the task as well as help them to see patterns more easily.
8. As students work together to fill in the chart on student page two, have them look for patterns. Some of these patterns may make their work easier. Tell students that they can save themselves a lot of work if they will stop and think mathematically. It normally takes a while, but usually someone in the class discovers that they only have to find the palindromes for half the numbers. The discovery occurs when they see that the palindrome they found for one number is the same for its reversed twin. For example, 12 and 21 both produce the palindrome 33 in one step, and 19 and 91 both produce the palindrome 121 in two steps.

## Procedure
1. Hand out student page one (if desired), and two copies of student page two to each student. Go over the concept of palindromes and the procedure for creating palindromic numbers as outlined in the instructions on page one.
2. Have students work together in groups to fill in the palindromes for the numbers from zero to 99. Encourage them to look for patterns to make their work easier.
3. When the all students have completed the charts on student page two, spend time as a whole class discussing the patterns discovered and the processes used to complete the charts.
4. Hand out student page three, as well as colored pens or pencils, to all students. Information from the charts on student page two will be used to complete this page. Students must first fill in the key, then complete the chart.
5. When everyone is finished with student page three, distribute student page four. Again, information from student page two is used to complete the chart.
6. After students have completed all four pages, go through the discussion questions as a class. You may also want to have students write about their palindromic discoveries or try some palindromic extensions.

## Connecting Learning
1. What did you discover about palindromes from this activity?
2. What kind of patterns did you see when you colored the boxes on student page three?
3. Do you think the patterns would continue if we were to go above 99? Why or why not?
4. Why do you think the most common palindrome for the numbers zero to 99 is 121?
5. Do you think 121 would be the most common palindrome for the numbers 100-200? Why or why not?

## Extensions
1. As a connection to literature and writing, have your students explore some palindromes that exist in language by creating palindromic words or sentences. You may want to read the palindromic story of Achilles, Tortoise and Crab, which can be read from beginning to end or end to beginning. (In *Gödel, Escher, Bach: An Eternal Golden Braid*, Douglas Hofstadter, 1979).
2. Find the palindromes for the numbers 100-199 (remembering that 196 has not been found to produce a palindrome).

## Solutions
The tables from each of the student pages, as well as some patterns that are present in these tables are given on the following page.

*Student page two*

| # | steps | palindrome | # | steps | palindrome |
|---|---|---|---|---|---|
| 00 | 0 | 00 | 50 | 1 | 55 |
| 01 | 1 | 11 | 51 | 1 | 66 |
| 02 | 1 | 22 | 52 | 1 | 77 |
| 03 | 1 | 33 | 53 | 1 | 88 |
| 04 | 1 | 44 | 54 | 1 | 99 |
| 05 | 1 | 55 | 55 | 0 | 55 |
| 06 | 1 | 66 | 56 | 1 | 121 |
| 07 | 1 | 77 | 57 | 2 | 363 |
| 08 | 1 | 88 | 58 | 2 | 484 |
| 09 | 1 | 99 | 59 | 3 | 1111 |
| 10 | 1 | 11 | 60 | 1 | 66 |
| 11 | 0 | 11 | 61 | 1 | 77 |
| 12 | 1 | 33 | 62 | 1 | 88 |
| 13 | 1 | 44 | 63 | 1 | 99 |
| 14 | 1 | 55 | 64 | 2 | 121 |
| 15 | 1 | 66 | 65 | 1 | 121 |
| 16 | 1 | 77 | 66 | 0 | 66 |
| 17 | 1 | 88 | 67 | 2 | 484 |
| 18 | 1 | 99 | 68 | 3 | 1111 |
| 19 | 2 | 121 | 69 | 4 | 4884 |
| 20 | 1 | 22 | 70 | 1 | 77 |
| 21 | 1 | 33 | 71 | 1 | 88 |
| 22 | 0 | 22 | 72 | 1 | 99 |
| 23 | 1 | 55 | 73 | 2 | 121 |
| 24 | 1 | 66 | 74 | 1 | 121 |
| 25 | 1 | 77 | 75 | 2 | 363 |
| 26 | 1 | 88 | 76 | 2 | 484 |
| 27 | 1 | 99 | 77 | 0 | 77 |
| 28 | 2 | 121 | 78 | 4 | 4884 |
| 29 | 1 | 121 | 79 | 6 | 44044 |
| 30 | 1 | 33 | 80 | 1 | 88 |
| 31 | 1 | 44 | 81 | 1 | 99 |
| 32 | 1 | 55 | 82 | 2 | 121 |
| 33 | 0 | 33 | 83 | 1 | 121 |
| 34 | 1 | 77 | 84 | 2 | 363 |
| 35 | 1 | 88 | 85 | 2 | 484 |
| 36 | 1 | 99 | 86 | 3 | 1111 |
| 37 | 2 | 121 | 87 | 4 | 4884 |
| 38 | 1 | 121 | 88 | 0 | 88 |
| 39 | 2 | 363 | 89 | 24 | 8813200023188 |
| 40 | 1 | 44 | 90 | 1 | 99 |
| 41 | 1 | 55 | 91 | 2 | 121 |
| 42 | 1 | 66 | 92 | 1 | 121 |
| 43 | 1 | 77 | 93 | 2 | 363 |
| 44 | 0 | 44 | 94 | 2 | 484 |
| 45 | 1 | 99 | 95 | 3 | 1111 |
| 46 | 2 | 121 | 96 | 4 | 4884 |
| 47 | 1 | 121 | 97 | 6 | 44044 |
| 48 | 2 | 363 | 98 | 24 | 8813200023188 |
| 49 | 2 | 484 | 99 | 0 | 99 |

*Student page four*

| Palindrome produced | Number of occurrences | Numbers that produce this palindrome |
|---|---|---|
| 11 | 3 | 01, 10, 11 |
| 22 | 3 | 02, 20, 22 |
| 33 | 5 | 03, 12, 21, 30, 33 |
| 44 | 5 | 04, 13, 31, 40, 44 |
| 55 | 7 | 05, 14, 41, 23, 32, 50, 55 |
| 66 | 7 | 06, 15, 51, 24, 42, 60, 66 |
| 77 | 9 | 07, 16, 61, 25, 52, 34, 43, 70, 77 |
| 88 | 9 | 08, 17, 71, 26, 62, 35, 53, 80, 88 |
| 99 | 11 | 09, 18, 81, 27, 72, 36, 63, 45, 54, 90, 99 |
| 121 | 16 | 19, 91, 28, 82, 29, 92, 37, 73, 38, 83, 46, 64, 47, 74, 56, 65 |
| 363 | 6 | 39, 93, 48, 84, 57, 75 |
| 484 | 6 | 49, 94, 67, 76, 78, 87 |
| 1111 | 4 | 59, 95, 68, 86 |
| 4884 | 4 | 69, 96, 78, 87 |
| 44044 | 2 | 79, 97 |
| 8813200023188 | 2 | 89, 98 |

*Patterns*

A few patterns present in this problem are listed below, but it is hoped that students' discoveries will go beyond what is presented here.

1. Zero-step palindromes (of two digits) occur every 11 numbers, beginning with 00 (00, 11, 22, 33, 44, etc.).
2. Any given number and its inverse will always produce the same palindrome in the same number of steps (i.e., 59 and 95 both produce 1111 in three steps).
3. When the numbers zero to 99 are arranged in a square, as on student page three, the numbers that can be made into palindromes in two through 24 steps all fall on parallel diagonals.
4. Several of the numbers that are already palindromes, when taken through the reversing and adding process, will produce some of the larger palindromes.

```
  11        33         55         77
 +11       +33        +55        +77
  22        66        110        154
 +22       +66       +011       +451
  44       132        121        605
 +44      +231       +121       +506
  88       363        242       1111
 +88      +363       +242
 176       726        484
+671      +627
 847      1353
+748     +3531
1595      4884
+5951
7546
+6457
14003
+30041
44044
```

*Student page three*

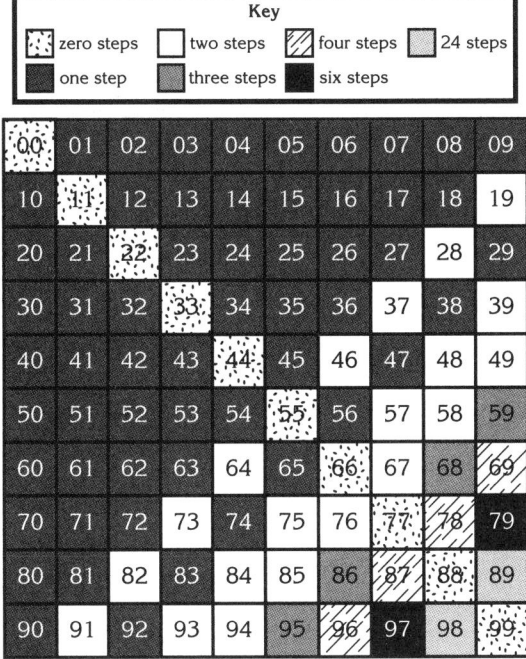

* Reprinted with permission from *Principles and Standards for School Mathematics*, 2000 by the National Council of Teachers of Mathematics. All rights reserved.

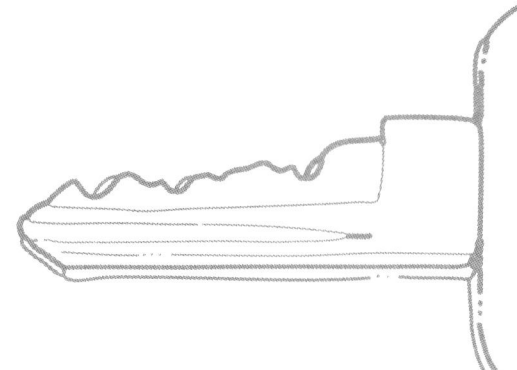

## Key Question

What patterns can you discover in palindromes?

## Learning Goal

**Students will:**

explore some of the fascinating properties and patterns that stem from the *palindrome conjecture.*

# PALINDROMIC PONDERINGS

Palindromes are words or numbers that are the same when read from left to right or from right to left. MOM and NOON are examples of palindromic words. The numbers 77, 252, and 1991 are examples of palindromic numbers.

Think of some other palindromic words and numbers. List them below.

---

Numbers that are not palindromes can be made into palindromes by reversing digits and adding. For example, 12 is not a palindrome, but if its digits are reversed to form 21 and the two numbers are added, the sum produced is the palindrome 33. Because it takes one reversal and addition to produce a palindrome from 12, we call it a one-step palindrome.

```
  12
+ 21
  33
```

Use the space to the right to find the palindrome for 13.

Sometimes, this reversing and adding takes more than one step. Look at the example below for 59, which is a three-step palindrome.

```
   59
 + 95
  154
 +451
  605
 +506
 1111
```

Use the space to the right to find the palindrome for 56. How many steps did it take?

Use this process of reversing and adding to find the palindromes for all the numbers from zero to 99. Numbers like 55 or 88 that are already palindromes should be recorded as zero-step palindromes. Record your information on the charts provided.

JUST FOR THE FUN OF IT! BOOK TWO © 2010 AIMS Education Foundation

Use this page to record your data.

| # | steps | palindrome |
|---|---|---|
|   |   |   |

| # | steps | palindrome |
|---|---|---|
|   |   |   |

What patterns do you notice? Do any of these patterns make your work easier? How?

# PALINDROMIC PONDERINGS

Complete the key below by filling in each box with a different color. Use the key to color in the chart showing how many steps it took to change each number into a palindrome.

## KEY

☐ zero steps  ☐ two steps  ☐ four steps  ☐ twenty-four steps
☐ one step   ☐ three steps ☐ six steps

| 00 | 01 | 02 | 03 | 04 | 05 | 06 | 07 | 08 | 09 |
| 10 | 11 | 12 | 13 | 14 | 15 | 16 | 17 | 18 | 19 |
| 20 | 21 | 22 | 23 | 24 | 25 | 26 | 27 | 28 | 29 |
| 30 | 31 | 32 | 33 | 34 | 35 | 36 | 37 | 38 | 39 |
| 40 | 41 | 42 | 43 | 44 | 45 | 46 | 47 | 48 | 49 |
| 50 | 51 | 52 | 53 | 54 | 55 | 56 | 57 | 58 | 59 |
| 60 | 61 | 62 | 63 | 64 | 65 | 66 | 67 | 68 | 69 |
| 70 | 71 | 72 | 73 | 74 | 75 | 76 | 77 | 78 | 79 |
| 80 | 81 | 82 | 83 | 84 | 85 | 86 | 87 | 88 | 89 |
| 90 | 91 | 92 | 93 | 94 | 95 | 96 | 97 | 98 | 99 |

JUST FOR THE FUN OF IT! BOOK TWO

Complete the chart below for all the palindromes with two or more digits. The first and last rows are done for you.

| Palindrome produced | Number of occurrences | Numbers that produce this palindrome |
|---|---|---|
| 11 | 3 | 01, 10, 11 |
|  |  |  |
|  |  |  |
|  |  |  |
|  |  |  |
|  |  |  |
|  |  |  |
|  |  |  |
|  |  |  |
|  |  |  |
|  |  |  |
|  |  |  |
|  |  |  |
|  |  |  |
|  |  |  |
|  |  |  |
| 8813200023188 | 2 | 89, 98 |

What patterns do you notice when, you look at palindromes this way?

# Connecting Learning

1. What did you discover about palindromes from this activity?

2. What kind of patterns did you see when you colored the boxes on student page three?

3. Do you think the patterns would continue if we were to go above 99? Why or why not?

4. Why do you think 121 is the most common palindrome for the numbers zero to 99?

5. Do you think 121 would be the most common palindrome for the numbers 100-200? Why or why not?

## Topic
Patterns

## Key Question
How can you decode and complete an addition chart when half of it is missing?

## Learning Goals
Students will:
* fill in the missing parts of a base-four addition table that is only partially complete, and
* discuss the patterns they discovered to allow them to do so.

## Guiding Documents
*Project 2061 Benchmark*
* *Mathematics is the study of many kinds of patterns, including numbers and shapes and operations on them. Sometimes patterns are studied because they help to explain how the world works or how to solve practical problems, sometimes because they are interesting in themselves.*

*NCTM Standards 2000\**
* *Describe, extend, and make generalizations about geometric and numeric patterns*
* *Build new mathematical knowledge through problem solving*

## Math
Math patterns
Number sense and numeration
One-to-one correspondence
Problem solving

## Integrated Processes
Observing
Comparing and contrasting
Interpreting data
Generalizing
Relating
Applying

## Problem-Solving Strategies
Look for patterns
Use logical thinking

## Materials
Student page

## Background Information
The late Nobel physicist Richard Feynman is the inspiration for this unusual activity. Feynman was an inveterate problem solver. He loved to play with problems and did them for the sheer fun of it, without much thought to their applications. In a PBS documentary that aired a few years after Feynman's death in 1988, one of the clips shows the great physicist telling the story of how he once tried to translate a Mayan codex. He explained that he knew that this codex had already been translated in the late 1800s by a German expert, but that he wanted to see if he could do it—just for the fun of it. Studying a copy of the codex, he discovered that some of the symbols were obviously numbers, and before long he had figured out the Mayan numeration system. In doing this, he noticed that the number 584 was repeated many times in the codex. This strange number puzzled him. Knowing that the Mayans were great observers of astronomical events, he went to the library at Cal Tech and discovered that 584 days is Venus' period in relation to the Earth (the time it takes Venus to appear again in exactly the same spot in our sky). In this way, Feynman described, he was able to begin to make sense of this interesting Mayan document. His enthusiasm in telling the story demonstrated that this activity was an enjoyable challenge, even though it was of dubious value. (Some might feel that Feynman's time would have been better spent working on some unsolved problem in physics rather than wasting time decoding a document that had already been translated.)

As the above story illustrates, Feynman enjoyed doing things just for the fun of it, without regard to their importance. This activity attempts to capture that same feeling. Hopefully your students will be drawn to this problem like Feynman was drawn to the Mayan codex.

## Management
1. The chart that your students will be deciphering and completing is actually a base-four addition table. Please DO NOT use this activity as a way to introduce or teach number bases to your students—that is not its intent. While it can be a good activity to use in conjunction with a study of number bases, its primary intent is to improve students' problem-solving skills as they look for patterns to help decode the chart.

## Procedure
1. Hand out the student page and go over the instructions. *Archaeologists have just unearthed some ancient clay tablets. One of these tablets seems to be a strange addition chart. Unfortunately, part of*

*the tablet is missing. Your challenge is to decipher the tablet and see if you can fill in the missing numbers.*

2. Have students work together in small groups to complete the table.
3. Close with a time of class discussion where students share the methods they used to decipher the tablet and any insights they gained while doing this problem.

### Connecting Learning
1. What did you find unusual about the tablet? [There are no numbers higher than three.]
2. What does this do to the answers to the addition problems? [Various. It changes them, they aren't "right," etc.]
3. What patterns did you notice in the addition table? (See *Solutions*.)
4. How did you go about filling in the missing numbers?
5. Did the patterns you discovered help you fill in the missing numbers?
6. How do you know that you are right?
7. What was hard about this problem?

### Extensions
1. Have students apply what they learned to "create" a base-five addition chart.
2. Challenge each group to come up with an addition (or subtraction) chart that is governed by a specific rule. Have them give an unfinished version to another group to see if their classmates can decipher the problem and complete the chart. For instance, one group might make an addition chart where three and eight are reversed. Another group might invent alternative symbols for numbers.

### Solutions
These solutions consist of some observations about the nature of the table as well as the answers to the completed table.

1. The only numbers in the table are zero, one, two, and three. This means that three is the highest possible one-digit number, 33 is the highest possible two-digit number, 333 is the highest possible three-digit number, etc. In this sense, the three can be equated with nine in a base-ten system.
2. In the first column, all of the answers are "right" (from a base-ten perspective). In the second column, every fourth answer is "wrong." In the third column, every third and fourth answer is "wrong." In the fourth column, every second, third and fourth answer is "wrong."
3. Because the table is written in base four, there are different place values than we are used to in base 10. The "ones" place has a value of one, the "tens" place has a value of four, the "hundreds" place has a value of 16, the "thousands" place has a value of 64, and so on.

* Reprinted with permission from *Principles and Standards for School Mathematics*, 2000 by the National Council of Teachers of Mathematics. All rights reserved.

### The completed addition table

| | | | |
|---|---|---|---|
| 0 + 0 = 0<br>0 + 1 = 1<br>0 + 2 = 2<br>0 + 3 = 3 | 1 + 0 = 1<br>1 + 1 = 2<br>1 + 2 = 3<br>1 + 3 = 10 | 2 + 0 = 2<br>2 + 1 = 3<br>2 + 2 = 10<br>2 + 3 = 11 | 3 + 0 = 3<br>3 + 1 = 10<br>3 + 2 = 11<br>3 + 3 = 12 |
| 10 + 0 = 10<br>10 + 1 = 11<br>10 + 2 = 12<br>10 + 3 = 13 | 11 + 0 = 11<br>11 + 1 = 12<br>11 + 2 = 13<br>11 + 3 = 20 | 12 + 0 = 12<br>12 + 1 = 13<br>12 + 2 = 20<br>12 + 3 = 21 | 13 + 0 = 13<br>13 + 1 = 20<br>13 + 2 = 21<br>13 + 3 = 22 |
| 20 + 0 = 20<br>20 + 1 = 21<br>20 + 2 = 22<br>20 + 3 = 23 | 21 + 0 = 21<br>21 + 1 = 22<br>21 + 2 = 23<br>21 + 3 = 30 | 22 + 0 = 22<br>22 + 1 = 23<br>22 + 2 = 30<br>22 + 3 = 31 | 23 + 0 = 23<br>23 + 1 = 30<br>23 + 2 = 31<br>23 + 3 = 32 |
| 30 + 0 = 30<br>30 + 1 = 31<br>30 + 2 = 32<br>30 + 3 = 33 | 31 + 0 = 31<br>31 + 1 = 32<br>31 + 2 = 33<br>31 + 3 = 100 | 32 + 0 = 32<br>32 + 1 = 33<br>32 + 2 = 100<br>32 + 3 = 101 | 33 + 0 = 33<br>33 + 1 = 100<br>33 + 2 = 101<br>33 + 3 = 102 |
| 100 + 0 = 100<br>100 + 1 = 101<br>100 + 2 = 102<br>100 + 3 = 103 | 101 + 0 = 101<br>101 + 1 = 102<br>101 + 2 = 103<br>101 + 3 = 110 | 102 + 0 = 102<br>102 + 1 = 103<br>102 + 2 = 110<br>102 + 3 = 111 | 103 + 0 = 103<br>103 + 1 = 110<br>103 + 2 = 111<br>103 + 3 = 112 |
| 110 + 0 = 110<br>110 + 1 = 111<br>110 + 2 = 112<br>110 + 3 = 113 | 111 + 0 = 111<br>111 + 1 = 112<br>111 + 2 = 113<br>111 + 3 = 120 | 112 + 0 = 112<br>112 + 1 = 113<br>112 + 2 = 120<br>112 + 3 = 121 | 113 + 0 = 113<br>113 + 1 = 120<br>113 + 2 = 121<br>113 + 3 = 122 |

...and so on

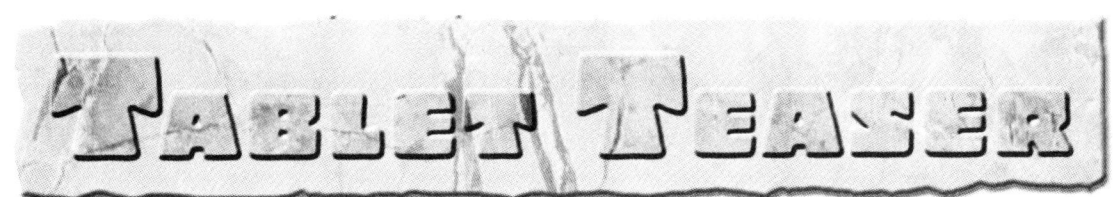

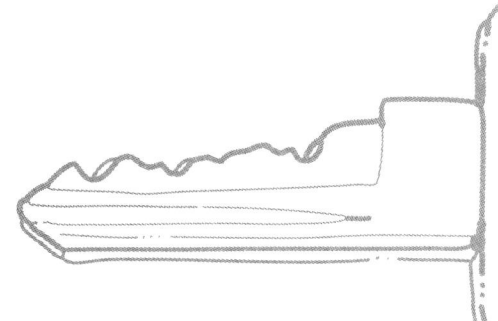

**Key Question**

How can you decode and complete an addition chart when half of it is missing?

## Learning Goals

**Students will:**

- fill in the missing parts of a base-four addition table that is only partially complete, and

- discuss the patterns they discovered to allow them to do so.

Archaeologists have just unearthed some ancient clay tablets. One of these tablets seems to be a strange addition chart. Unfortunately, part of the tablet is missing.

Your challenge is to decipher the tablet and see if you can fill in the missing numbers.

0 + 0 = 0
0 + 1 = 1
0 + 2 = 2
0 + 3 = 3

1 + 0 = 1
1 + 1 = 2
1 + 2 = 3
1 + 3 = 10

2 + 0 = 2
2 + 1 = 3
2 + 2 = 10
2 + 3 = 11

3 + 0 = 3
3 + 1 = 10
3 + 2 = 11
3 + 3 = 12

10 + 0 = 10
10 + 1 = 11
10 + 2 = 12
10 + 3 = 13

11 + 0 = 11
11 + 1 = 12
11 + 2 = 13
11 + 3 = 20

12 + 0 = 12
12 + 1 = 13
12 + 2 = 20
12 + 3 = 21

13 + 0 = 13
13 + 1 = 20
13 + 2 = 21
13 + 3 = 22

20 + 0 = 20
20 + 1 = 21
20 + 2 = 22
20 + 3 = 23

21 + 0 = 21
21 + 1 = 22
21 + 2 = 23
21 + 3 = 30

22 + 0 = 22
22 + 1 = 23
22 + 2 =

23 +

30 + 0 = 30
30 + 1 = 31
30 + 2 = 32
30 + 3 = 33

31 + 0 = 31
31 + 1 = 32
31
3

100 + 0 = 100
100 + 1 =
100
10

1

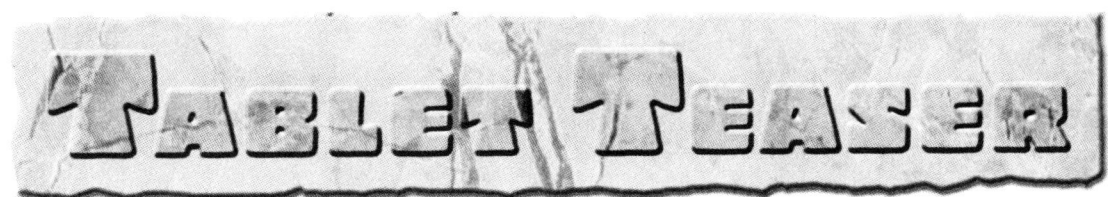

## Connecting Learning

1. What did you find unusual about the tablet?

2. What does this do to the answers to the addition problems?

3. What patterns did you notice in the addition table?

4. How did you go about filling in the missing numbers?

5. Did the patterns you discovered help you fill in the missing numbers?

6. How do you know that you are right?

7. What was hard about this problem?

# Mind Reader's Magic Cards

**Topic**
Problem solving

**Key Question**
How can you guess what number from one to 15 someone else is thinking of if they tell you on which of four cards it appears?

**Learning Goals**
Students will:
- play a game with magic cards many times,
- complete charts that make patterns in the card game easier to see, and
- try to understand and explain the secret of the magic cards.

**Guiding Documents**
*Project 2061 Benchmark*
- *Mathematics is the study of many kinds of patterns, including numbers and shapes and operations on them. Sometimes patterns are studied because they help to explain how the world works or how to solve practical problems, sometimes because they are interesting in themselves.*

*NCTM Standards 2000\**
- *Describe, extend, and make generalizations about geometric and numeric patterns*
- *Build new mathematical knowledge through problem solving*
- *Solve problems that arise in mathematics and in other contexts*

**Math**
Math patterns
Problem solving

**Integrated Processes**
Observing
Comparing and contrasting
Inferring
Generalizing

**Problem-Solving Strategies**
Organize the information
Use logical thinking
Look for patterns

**Materials**
Colored pencils or crayons
Enlarged *Magic Cards*
Strips of paper—2" x 8" (see *Solutions*)
Student pages

**Background Information**
This activity is designed to be used in conjunction with *Standing Invitation* and *Binary Bemusements*. It should be done first to introduce students to the concept of magic cards, which are based on the binary number system. It can be followed by *Standing Invitation* for an expansion on the magic cards idea, and *Binary Bemusements* for a more in-depth look at binary numbers.

*Mind Reader's Magic Cards* is a simple version of a "mind reading" game that has been around in recreational mathematics for years. In the typical version, there are five cards used to play a game in which a "mind reader" (a person who knows the cards' secret) shows the cards to a player (someone who doesn't know the secret) and asks him or her to think of a number from one to 31. The mind reader tells the player that s/he can guess the number correctly if told on which of the cards the chosen number appears. When the mind reader is given this information, s/he immediately tells the player the correct number. This is done by quickly adding the first number on each card chosen. This works because the first number on each card represents one of the binary number system's place value groupings (16s, eights, fours, twos, and ones) used to make the player's number. For example, 23 appears on the cards with 16, four, two, and one in the top left corners, because these numbers add up to 23.

In this simplified version of the mind reading game, there are only four cards instead of five, but the same principles apply. Through this activity, students will discover the secret of the magic cards and gain insights that will enable them to better understand the binary system.

**Management**
1. This activity is split into two parts—a whole-class section and an independent/group section. In the first section you will play the mind reading game together as a class, guessing the numbers chosen by students. In the second section, the students will attempt to understand the secret of the magic cards by playing the game with classmates and looking for patterns.

JUST FOR THE FUN OF IT! BOOK TWO © 2010 AIMS Education Foundation

2. To introduce this activity, you will need make a set of magic cards that are large enough to be seen by the entire class when held up at the front of the room. You can enlarge the cards given on student page one, or you can make your own. If you make your own, be sure to use the numbers and colors indicated on the student page.
3. When playing the game as a class, there may be students who already know the secret. If there are, ask them not to give the secret away and have them help you guess the other students' numbers.
4. Students will need either colored pencils or crayons to do their work on the student pages. The colors they will need are red, green, yellow, and blue.
5. The second part of the activity can be done in a couple of ways. You may want to have students work independently on the student pages, or you may choose to have students work in groups. Decide which method is most appropriate for your class.
6. Before you present this activity, you will need to decide what to do when students discover the secret (or what to do if no one discovers it). If one student, or group of students, tells the rest of the class the secret, it robs others of the opportunity to discover the secret on their own. If no one discovers it, however, the frustration level might suggest working together as a whole class to come up with a method.
7. Although students will not be picking it as one of the secret numbers, zero is included on the table they color in. Without zero, the patterns in the table would not be consistent.

## Procedure
*Whole-Class Section*
1. Introduce the activity by showing students your large magic cards and telling them that you can discover the number (from one to 15) they are thinking of if they tell you what cards the number is on. Ask if any of the students have played this game before. *If some already know the secret, ask them not to give it away and tell them they can help you guess other students' numbers.*
2. Play several games with the class before challenging students to discover the secret of the magic cards.

*Independent/Group Section*
1. Hand out the student pages and colored pencils (or crayons).
2. Have students color the cards and the chart, and answer the questions as they look for patterns.
3. As students begin to discover the secret to the magic cards, have them try playing games with their peers to practice their mind-reading skills.
4. Close with a time of class discussion where you share the patterns discovered in the numbers and have students offer explanations for how to read someone's mind using the magic cards.

## Connecting Learning
1. Did you discover the secret of the magic cards? [Hopefully all of your students will have been able to discover a way to guess someone else's number.]
2. How can you know what number someone has chosen? [By adding up the first numbers of the cards it is on, by looking at the chart with the colors, etc.]
3. What patterns did you discover in the numbers that appear on each of the cards? (See *Solutions*.)
4. What do these patterns have to do with the way the magic cards work? (See *Solutions*.)

## Extension
Have students make a set of magic cards for the numbers one to 31 following the patterns that they have already discovered and trying to infer what the patterns for the next card would be. Extension pages one and two are for this activity. (See *Solutions*.)

## Solutions
The easiest way to guess a person's number is to add the first number(s) on the card(s) on which it appears. For example, if the number is 7, it appears on Cards B, C, and D. The first numbers on these cards are 4, 2, and 1, so the number is guessed by adding these numbers (4 + 2 + 1 = 7).

Another way to guess the number is to use a process of elimination. There are a number of ways to do this. One possible method is described here. The mind reader asks a series of questions. The first question is if the number is on Card A. If the answer is yes, then the number must be one of the numbers 8-15. If not, it must be one of the numbers 0-7. This cuts the number of possibilities in half, leaving only eight. The next question the reader asks is if the number is on Card D. If the answer is yes, the number is odd; if no, the number is even. This second question cuts the remaining numbers in half, leaving only four. The next question is if the number is on Card B, which cuts the remaining numbers in half leaving only two possibilities. The final question is if the number is on Card C, which determines which of the two remaining possibilities is the correct number.

Yet another way to guess the number is to use the colored-in chart and two strips of paper. The mind reader again asks a series of four questions that determine which cards the number is on and uses the strips of paper to cover the eliminated numbers. (In this method, the questions must go in order from Card A to B to C to D.) To illustrate how this works, consider the number 11. The first question ascertains that it is on Card A, which allows the uncolored numbers (0-7) to be covered up. The next question determines that it is not on Card B, which allows the colored numbers (12-15) to be covered. The next question determines that it is on Card C, allowing the uncolored numbers

8 and 9 to be covered. The final question shows that it is on Card D, allowing the uncolored 10 to be covered and leaving 11 as the answer.

The reason the magic cards work is because they are based on the binary system, which uses the powers of two. The numbers in the top left corner of each card are the powers of two: Card D, $1 = 2^0$; Card C, $2 = 2^1$; Card B, $4 = 2^2$; and Card A, $8 = 2^3$. Using these numbers—one, two, four, and eight—it is possible to make every number from one to 15 in a unique way by adding them in some combination.

| Number | Combination that creates the number | Card(s) on which the number appears |
|---|---|---|
| 1 | 1 | Card D |
| 2 | 2 | Card C |
| 3 | 2 + 1 | Cards C & D |
| 4 | 4 | Card B |
| 5 | 4 + 1 | Cards B & D |
| 6 | 4 + 2 | Cards B & C |
| 7 | 4 + 2 + 1 | Cards B, C, & D |
| 8 | 8 | Card A |
| 9 | 8 + 1 | Cards A & D |
| 10 | 8 + 2 | Cards A & C |
| 11 | 8 + 2 + 1 | Cards A, C, & D |
| 12 | 8 + 4 | Cards A & B |
| 13 | 8 + 4 + 1 | Cards A, B, & D |
| 14 | 8 + 4 + 2 | Cards A, B, & C |
| 15 | 8 + 4 + 2 + 1 | Cards A, B, C, & D |

As you can see, each number from one to 15 appears only on the card(s) that has(have) the number(s) that must be added to create it. Therefore, adding the numbers in the top left corner of the card(s) on which an unknown number occurs will give you that number every time.

To create a set of five magic cards that will work for the numbers one to 31 *(Extension),* the same principle applies. The number at the top left corner of the fifth card will be $2^4$, or 16. Only numbers that have 16 in their sum will be on that card. If done properly, your magic cards for the numbers one to 31 should look like this:

```
   Card A         Card B         Card C         Card D         Card E
16 17 18 19    8  9 10 11    4  5  6  7    2  3  6  7    1  3  5  7
20 21 22 23   12 13 14 15   12 13 14 15   10 11 14 15    9 11 13 15
24 25 26 27   24 25 26 27   20 21 22 23   18 19 22 23   17 19 21 23
28 29 30 31   28 29 30 31   28 29 30 31   26 27 30 31   25 27 29 31
```

\* Reprinted with permission from *Principles and Standards for School Mathematics,* 2000 by the National Council of Teachers of Mathematics. All rights reserved.

## Key Question

How can you guess what number from one to 15 someone else is thinking of if they tell you on which of four cards it appears?

## Learning Goals

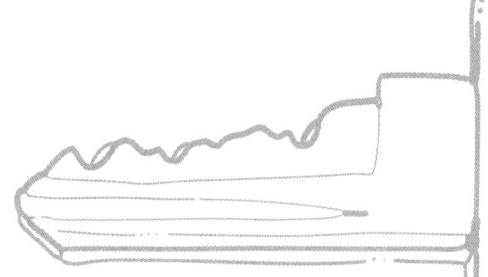

- play a game with magic cards many times,

- complete charts that make patterns in the card game easier to see, and

- try to understand and explain the secret of the magic cards.

# Mind Reader's MAGIC CARDS

Think of a number from one to 15. See which of the cards below has your number written on it. If you tell your teacher the card(s) your number is on, s/he will immediately tell you your number.

How does s/he do this?

Can you discover the secret of the magic cards?

**Card A**
8 9 10
11 12
13 14 15
[Red]

**Card B**
4 5 6 7
12 13 14 15
[Green]

**Card C**
2 3 6 7
10 11 14 15
[Yellow]

**Card D**
1 3 5
7 9 11
13 15
[Blue]

JUST FOR THE FUN OF IT! BOOK TWO © 2010 AIMS Education Foundation

# Mind Reader's Magic Cards

The chart below may help you discover the secret of the magic cards. Use the color indicated under each card to fill in the boxes that correspond with the numbers on that card.

| # | Card A<br>8 9 10 11<br>12 13 14 15<br>(Red) | Card B<br>4 5 6 7<br>12 13 14 15<br>(Green) | Card C<br>2 3 6 7<br>10 11 14 15<br>(Yellow) | Card D<br>1 3 5 7<br>9 11 13 15<br>(Blue) |
|---|---|---|---|---|
| 0 | | | | |
| 1 | | | | |
| 2 | | | | |
| 3 | | | | |
| 4 | | | | |
| 5 | | | | |
| 6 | | | | |
| 7 | | | | |
| 8 | | | | |
| 9 | | | | |
| 10 | | | | |
| 11 | | | | |
| 12 | | | | |
| 13 | | | | |
| 14 | | | | |
| 15 | | | | |

What patterns do you see in the table?

Can you use the chart to find someone else's number? How?

Try your method and see if it works.

# MORE MAGIC CARDS
## (Extension)

Now that you have discovered the patterns that exist for each magic card, you are ready to add another card to your set. The chart on the next page has empty spaces on each card in which to write the appropriate numbers. You will have to use the patterns that you discovered for the numbers one to 15 to help you as you fill in the numbers 16-31. Be sure to write the missing numbers on each card as well as color the spaces beneath the cards with the appropriate color. Fill in the chart before answering these questions.

1. How did you know which numbers to put on each card?

2. Why were the numbers 16-31 added when another magic card was added?

3. What numbers do you think would be used if a sixth magic card were added? How do you know?

Once you have completed your magic card chart and answered the above questions, create a second set of magic cards that include the new card you added. See if you can use the method that you developed for four cards to guess someone's number now that there are five cards.

4. What method did you use to find someone's number now that there are five magic cards?

5. Is it the same method that you used for four magic cards? Why or why not?

JUST FOR THE FUN OF IT! BOOK TWO

# MORE MAGIC CARDS (Extension)

Fill in the table below with the numbers that belong on each card. Color the appropriate spaces with the color indicated.

| # | Card A<br>_ _ _<br>_ _ _<br>_ _ _<br>[Orange] | Card B<br>8 9 10 11<br>12 13 14 15<br>_ _<br>[Red] | Card C<br>4 5 6 7<br>12 13 14 15<br>_ _<br>[Green] | Card D<br>2 3 6 7<br>10 11 14 15<br>_ _<br>[Yellow] | Card E<br>1 3 5 7<br>9 11 13 15<br>_ _<br>[Blue] |
|---|---|---|---|---|---|
| 16 | | | | | |
| 17 | | | | | |
| 18 | | | | | |
| 19 | | | | | |
| 20 | | | | | |
| 21 | | | | | |
| 22 | | | | | |
| 23 | | | | | |
| 24 | | | | | |
| 25 | | | | | |
| 26 | | | | | |
| 27 | | | | | |
| 28 | | | | | |
| 29 | | | | | |
| 30 | | | | | |
| 31 | | | | | |

## Connecting Learning

1. Did you discover the secret of the magic cards?

2. How can you know what number someone has chosen?

3. What patterns did you discover in the numbers that appear on each of the cards?

4. What do these patterns have to do with the way the magic cards work?

# Standing Invitation

**Topic**
Math patterns

**Key Question**
How can you make the numbers zero to 15 using combinations of the numbers one, two, four, and eight?

**Learning Goals**
Students will:
• learn that all of the numbers from zero to 15 can be made by adding some combination of one, two, four, and eight;
• find patterns in the solutions; and
• explore the binary system, if appropriate.

**Guiding Documents**
*Project 2061 Benchmark*
• Mathematics is the study of many kinds of patterns, including numbers and shapes and operations on them. Sometimes patterns are studied because they help to explain how the world works or how to solve practical problems, sometimes because they are interesting in themselves.

*NCTM Standards 2000\**
• Describe, extend, and make generalizations about geometric and numeric patterns
• Build new mathematical knowledge through problem solving
• Solve problems that arise in mathematics and in other contexts

**Math**
Math patterns
Problem solving

**Integrated Processes**
Observing
Inferring
Generalizing

**Problem-Solving Strategies**
Look for patterns
Organize the information
Use logical thinking

**Materials**
Card stock
Colored pencils or crayons
Student pages

**Background Information**
This activity can be done by a wide range of ages with different levels of sophistication to study different things. Younger children can look for the patterns that exist in the number combinations, while older children can begin to understand the more difficult concepts behind those patterns. *Standing Invitation* works because of the binary number system, which uses zeros and ones to represent positive whole numbers. While this activity does not deal specifically with binary numbers, it is a good introduction for a study of the base-two system.

**Management**
1. This activity is intended to follow *Mind Reader's Magic Cards*.
2. This activity is divided into whole-class and small-group times. A majority of the activity time should be spent on the whole-class section to ensure that all students have fully grasped the concept of making the numbers from zero to 15 with eight, four, two, and one. Be sure not to rush over this section of the activity.
3. You will need to prepare four cards ahead of time for the whole-class portion of this activity. Make a copy of the page provided with pictures of the families. You may want to enlarge it a bit so they are easier to see. Color the clothes of the Octovians red and then glue the picture to a piece of card stock. Color the Forsythes green, the Doubletons yellow, and Steven Singleham blue. Glue each of these groups to a separate piece of card stock. These cards will be used by you and the students during the invitation game.
4. There is an explanation of the invitation game included with the student pages that can be displayed using a projection device or simply verbalized by you as you explain the game.
5. Students will need crayons or colored pencils to complete student page one. They will each need the colors red, yellow, green, and blue.
6. This activity has many potential extensions suited for older children that explore the binary system in

a deeper, more significant way. Depending on the age of your students, you may or may not want to include a discussion of the binary system in the basic activity. Because the patterns in the problem all stem from the fact that the binary system is a base-two system, a discussion is not out of order, but younger students may have a difficult time grasping the concept of a binary system.

**Procedure**
*Whole-Class: Section One*
1. At the front of the room, display the four family cards you prepared so that they can be seen clearly by all students. The card with the Octovians goes on the left (from the viewer's perspective), with the others placed to its right in descending order. Tell the students that these children are from very close families. Whenever one is invited anywhere, all of the family goes along. The only exception is Steven Singleham, who is an only child. Ask the students how they could invite exactly six friends to a party. Hopefully, they will see that they could invite the Forsythes and the Doubletons to have exactly six friends at their party (if they say to invite six of the Octovians, remind them that the families always stick together).
2. Repeat this process with other numbers from zero to 15. Make sure that students have enough exposure with this introductory section to see that each number between zero and 15 can be made with various combinations of the four families (or no families, in the case of zero).

*Whole-Class: Section Two*
1. Set up four chairs in front of the class, facing the students. Have four volunteers come and sit in the chairs.
2. Give each student one of the family cards, keeping them in the same order as above—Octovians on the left (as seen by the class), followed by the Forsythes, the Doubletons, and Steven Singleham.
3. Tell the volunteers you need their help in deciding which families to invite to your party—when they hear how many people you want to invite, they need to stand up and show the card they are holding if their family should be included in the invitation. (If you wish, you may display the invitation game explanation at this point.) For example, if you tell them you want to invite five friends, the student with the Forsythes and the student with Steven Singleham should stand up and show their cards.
4. Repeat this process several times with other numbers from zero to 15 until the volunteers have had enough practice to become somewhat comfortable with the process.
5. Once students are comfortable, tell them that you are going to play a game. In the game you will count slowly from zero to 15 and they will stand up and show their cards for each number that uses their family. Play this game several times.
6. After several runs, thank the first volunteers and ask for new ones. Make sure the new students sit in the proper order and have them do the same thing while counting slowly from zero to 15.
7. After a few groups of volunteers have tried, have everyone sit down and conduct a time of class discussion where students share the patterns they noticed in the game.
8. If you wish, you may have one or two other groups of students come to the front to see how fast they can make the numbers zero to 15. Have them verbalize the patterns before they return to their seats.

*Small-Group Section*
1. Have students get into groups and hand out the student pages.
2. Make sure everyone understands the instructions, and give students sufficient time to complete both pages. *The characters in the chart below are in groups of eight, four, two, and one according to their families. Color the Octovians red, the Forsythes green, the Doubletons yellow, and Steven Singleham blue. Show which families you would use to make each of the numbers from zero to 15. Do this by filling the boxes with the appropriate colors.*
3. Close the activity with a final time of discussion where students share any additional patterns they discovered in the problem.

**Connecting Learning**
*Whole-Class: Section Two*
1. What patterns have you noticed in this game? [The person with Steven Singleham is up on the odd numbers, the person with the Octovians doesn't stand up until the last eight, etc.]
2. Can you explain any of these patterns?
3. Did you notice anything else while everyone was playing this game?

*Small-Group Section*
1. Did you find any more patterns when you filled out the charts that you didn't see in the game?
2. What are the patterns?
3. Why do you think we have been using the numbers eight, four, two, and one? [The game is based on the binary system, which uses the powers of two. $1 = 2^0$, $2 = 2^1$, $4 = 2^2$, $8 = 2^3$]
4. Would the game work if we used different numbers? [Not unless you were using other powers of two to create numbers greater than one to 15, or powers of another number, such as three or four.]

5. Why or why not? [It would not be possible to create all of the numbers from one to 15 using a unique combination each time.]

**Extensions**
1. For older students, you can include a discussion of the way a computer uses the binary system to function. The invitation game played in *Whole-Class: Section Two* can be seen as a model of a simple computer that can count from zero to 15. Whenever a student is standing, the computer reads that as a one, and when they are sitting, the computer reads a zero.
2. Expand the problem to include the numbers one to 31 by adding a family with 16 children (16 = $2^4$) and have students explore the patterns.
3. Follow this activity with *Binary Bemusements.* If your students are not advanced enough to do *Binary Bemusements,* but you would still like to have a discussion of the binary system, extension pages one and two can be used for this purpose.

**Solutions**
This section describes the patterns that your students will hopefully notice for the different families.
1. Steven Singleham (one) is used on all of the odd numbers.
2. The Doubletons (two) are used twice in a row, every two numbers beginning with two.
3. The Forsythes (four) are used four times in a row every four numbers beginning with four.
4. The Octovians (eight) are used eight times in a row, beginning with the number eight.

The reasons for these patterns have to do with the binary number system, which is examined in greater depth in *Binary Bemusements.*

\* Reprinted with permission from *Principles and Standards for School Mathematics,* 2000 by the National Council of Teachers of Mathematics. All rights reserved.

## Key Question

How can you make the numbers zero to 15 using combinations of the numbers one, two, four, and eight?

## Learning Goals

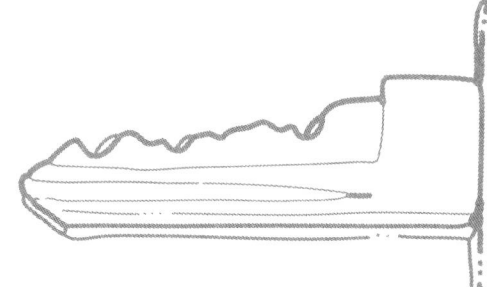

- learn that all of the numbers from zero to 15 can be made by adding some combination of one, two, four, and eight;

- find patterns in the solutions; and

- explore the binary system, if appropriate.

# Standing Invitation

Steven **Singleham**

The **Doubletons**

The **Forsythes**

The **Octovians**

# Standing Invitation

## The Invitation Game:

The families in our town are a little eccentric. If you invite one of the family members, all of the others will come as well, so inviting one Octovian is the same as inviting eight! We're going to have a party, but our mother keeps changing her mind about how many people we can invite. Every time she changes her mind, we have to change which families we ask to the party. Help us make up our guest list. As your teacher calls out a number of people to be invited, stand up if the family you are holding should be included in the invitation.

# The OCTOVIANS

# Standing Invitation

The characters in the chart below are in groups of eight, four, two, and one according to their families. Color the Octovians red, the Forsythes green, the Doubletons yellow, and Steven Singleham blue. Show which families you would use to make each of the numbers from zero to 15. Do this by filling the boxes with the appropriate colors. For example, five is made with the Forsythes and Steven Singleham, so color the fifth row box under the Forsythes green and the fifth row box under Steven Singleham blue. Leave the fifth row boxes under the Octovians and the Doubletons blank. Use your colored pencils or crayons to complete this chart, then answer the questions on the next page.

| # | (Octovians) | (Forsythes) | (Doubletons) | (Singleham) |
|---|---|---|---|---|
| 0 | | | | |
| 1 | | | | |
| 2 | | | | |
| 3 | | | | |
| 4 | | | | |
| 5 | | | | |
| 6 | | | | |
| 7 | | | | |
| 8 | | | | |
| 9 | | | | |
| 10 | | | | |
| 11 | | | | |
| 12 | | | | |
| 13 | | | | |
| 14 | | | | |
| 15 | | | | |

JUST FOR THE FUN OF IT! BOOK TWO © 2010 AIMS Education Foundation

# Standing Invitation

1. There are many interesting patterns to be found on the chart. Look at the column with Steven Singleham. What pattern(s) do you notice?

2. What pattern(s) do you notice in the column with the Doubletons?

3. What about the column with the Forsythes?

4. What pattern(s) do the Octovians make?

5. Compare this chart with the one from *Mind Reader's Magic Cards*. What connections do you see between the two activities?

JUST FOR THE FUN OF IT! BOOK TWO

# Standing Invitation
## Binary System Fact Sheet

The activity you have just done is based on binary numbers. In the binary system, there are only two digits with which to write numbers—0 and 1. However, using only these two digits in a way similar to what you have done today, it is possible to write all of the positive whole numbers.

The binary system is a base-two system, which is why it only uses the numbers 0 and 1. The 0s and 1s in binary stand for the different powers of two, depending on where they are in the number. The powers of two are: 1 ($2^0$), 2 ($2^1$), 4 ($2^2$), 8 ($2^3$), 16 ($2^4$), etc.

If there is a 0 in a binary number, it means that you do not count that power of two in the total. If there is a 1, it means that you do count that power of two in your total. Working from right to left, the places stand for $2^0$, $2^1$, $2^2$, $2^3$, and so on. For example, to read the binary number 1011, you would add $2^3 + 0 + 2^1 + 2^0$, which is 11.

0 = Not counted in total
1 = Counted in total

| Eights Place | Fours Place | Twos Place | Ones Place |
|---|---|---|---|
| $2^3$ | $2^2$ | $2^1$ | $2^0$ |
| (8) | (4) | (2) | (1) |
| 1 | 0 | 1 | 1 |

$8 + 2 + 1 = 11$

Using only these four places, 15 is the largest number that is possible because $8 + 4 + 2 + 1 = 15$. However, if you added $2^4$ to the chart on the far left (the sixteen's place), you would be able to get numbers larger than 15.

Now that you understand a little bit about the binary system, try to fill in the chart on the next page, writing all of the numbers from zero to 15 in binary.

Fill in the chart below using the binary system. Remember, a 1 means that you **are** counting the value of that place in the total, and a 0 means that you **are not** counting the value of that place in the total. The number 11 is done for you as an example.

| # | EIGHTS $2^3$ | FOURS $2^2$ | TWOS $2^1$ | ONES $2^0$ |
|---|---|---|---|---|
| 0 | | | | |
| 1 | | | | |
| 2 | | | | |
| 3 | | | | |
| 4 | | | | |
| 5 | | | | |
| 6 | | | | |
| 7 | | | | |
| 8 | | | | |
| 9 | | | | |
| 10 | | | | |
| 11 | 1 | 0 | 1 | 1 |
| 12 | | | | |
| 13 | | | | |
| 14 | | | | |
| 15 | | | | |

**Extra Challenge:** Write the numbers 16-20 using the binary system on the back of this paper.

## Connecting Learning

*Whole-Class: Section Two*

1. What patterns have you noticed in this game?

2. Can you explain any of these patterns?

3. Did you notice anything else while everyone was playing this game?

# Connecting Learning

*Small-Group Section*

1. Did you find any more patterns when you filled out the charts that you didn't see in the game?

2. What are the patterns?

3. Why do you think we have been using the numbers eight, four, two, and one?

4. Would the game work if we used different numbers?

5. Why or why not?

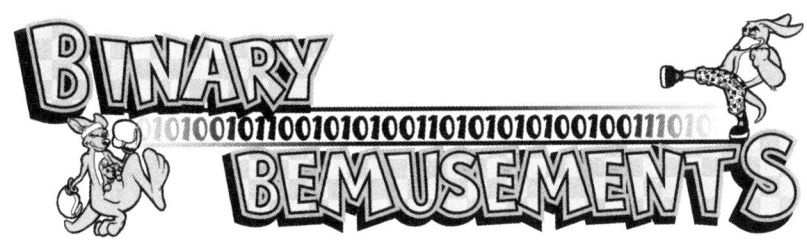

## Topic
Binary numbers

## Key Question
What are number bases, and how do our number cards—which are based on the binary system—work?

## Learning Goals
Students will
- expand their knowledge of the binary number system by creating and explaining binary number cards, and
- gain a basic understanding of other number bases.

## Guiding Documents
*Project 2061 Benchmark*
- *Numbers can be represented using sequences of only two symbols (such as 1 and 0, on and off); computers work this way.*

*NCTM Standards 2000\**
- *Build new mathematical knowledge through problem solving*
- *Create and use representations to organize, record, and communicate mathematical ideas*

## Math
Number bases
Powers of two
Binary numbers
Problem solving

## Integrated Processes
Observing
Relating
Generalizing

## Problem-Solving Strategies
Look for patterns
Organize the information

## Materials
Unlined 4" x 6" index cards, 16 per student
Jumbo paper clips, one per student
Scissors
Hole punch
Student pages

## Background Information
This activity builds on the concept of binary numbers that is developed in *Mind Reader's Magic Cards* and *Standing Invitation*. It takes the factual knowledge gained in those activities, and has students translate that into a physical application. This makes the concept of binary numbers more meaningful by giving students a tangible model of the base-two system. *Binary Bemusements* assumes that students already have a basic understanding of the binary system; it should not be used as an introduction to binary numbers.

Because this activity requires a more complete understanding of the binary system, it is geared toward middle school students or very advanced upper elementary students. In order to do this activity, students must be able to deal with the concepts of powers. Since they are dealing with the binary system, the students will be using the powers of two in this case. Although the explanation is not a part of this activity, students should understand why $2^0 = 1$, $2^1 = 2$, $2^2 = 4$ and so on.

## Management
1. This activity is intended to follow *Mind Reader's Magic Cards* and *Standing Invitation*. It is strongly recommended that students complete both of those activities before doing this one.
2. For this activity, each student will be making 16 binary cards. These cards work well if they are made from unlined 4" x 6" index cards. Punch four equally-spaced holes along the top of each card using a ¼" hole punch. These holes should be close to the top, but not so close that they will easily rip. Since students will be cutting these cards and may make some mistakes, have some extra cards on hand. As an alternative to index cards, tagboard or card stock cut to a similar size will also work.
3. This activity requires students to deal with some advanced concepts that even adults may find challenging. Because of this, you should make sure your students have at least a basic understanding of exponents and number systems before tackling this activity. The first student page covers some of this material, but students must already have a base of knowledge from which to work.
4. You should make a set of working binary cards for yourself that you can use as a demonstration when introducing this activity. You may wish to

JUST FOR THE FUN OF IT! BOOK TWO © 2010 AIMS Education Foundation

make these larger than the student versions so that they are easier for the class to see.
5. You may want to display the answer keys in the *Solutions* section using a projection device so that students can check their work at each stage before moving on to the next step. Just one mistake on one of the student pages will lead to binary cards that will not work as they are supposed to.

**Procedure**
1. Distribute student page one and spend some time going over the information as a class, helping students fill out the chart, and making sure that they understand the concepts presented.
2. Hand out student pages two and three, and allow students to work in groups to fill in the information. It is critical that the answers on student page three are correct, or students will not be able to make their binary cards properly. Before handing out the next student page, make sure that all groups have correctly written the numbers from zero to 15 in binary (an answer key is included in the *Solutions* section).
3. Give students the fourth page, scissors, and pre-punched index cards. Introduce this section by showing the class your set of binary cards and how they arrange themselves in numerical order. Be sure to review the instructions, perhaps making one card as a class to ensure that everyone understands the task.
4. Allow students to work in groups or by themselves to make and test their binary cards.
5. When everyone has had sufficient time to make their cards, hand out student page five and have students answer the questions.
6. Close with a time of class discussion and sharing.

**Connecting Learning**
1. What did you learn about the base-two system from this activity?
2. Why do your binary cards work?
3. Do you think you could make a binary card for the number 16?
4. How would it look?
5. Why do you have to move your pencil from right to left to put the cards in order?
6. What are you wondering now?

**Extensions**
1. Have students make binary cards for the numbers zero to 31.
2. Challenge students to write the numbers from one to 15 in other number bases such as base three, four, and five.
3. Instead of putting their cards in numerical order, have students try to pick out a given card from the deck. Extension pages one and two give both a teacher's guide and a student page for this activity.

**Solutions**
The following pages give the answer keys for the student pages, as well as a visual check for how each binary card should look. If necessary, you can make a copy of any or all of the pages for students to use as a check on their work. However, if you choose to do this, be sure that the keys are used as a check, and not to fill in the tables or make the cards.

* Reprinted with permission from *Principles and Standards for School Mathematics*, 2000 by the National Council of Teachers of Mathematics. All rights reserved.

# Key for student page one

| One-Number Combinations | Total |
|---|---|
| 1 | 1 |
| 2 | 2 |
| 4 | 4 |
| 8 | 8 |
| Two-Number Combinations | |
| 2, 1 | 3 |
| 4, 1 | 5 |
| 8, 1 | 9 |
| 4, 2 | 6 |
| 8, 2 | 10 |
| 8, 4 | 12 |
| Three-Number Combinations | |
| 4, 2, 1 | 7 |
| 8, 2, 1 | 11 |
| 8, 4, 2 | 14 |
| Four-Number Combinations | |
| 8, 4, 2, 1 | 15 |

# Key for student page two

| | $2^3$ | $2^2$ | $2^1$ | $2^0$ | | $2^3$ | $2^2$ | $2^1$ | $2^0$ |
|---|---|---|---|---|---|---|---|---|---|
| 0 | 0 | 0 | 0 | 0 | 8  | 1 | 0 | 0 | 0 |
| 1 | 0 | 0 | 0 | 1 | 9  | 1 | 0 | 0 | 1 |
| 2 | 0 | 0 | 1 | 0 | 10 | 1 | 0 | 1 | 0 |
| 3 | 0 | 0 | 1 | 1 | 11 | 1 | 0 | 1 | 1 |
| 4 | 0 | 1 | 0 | 0 | 12 | 1 | 1 | 0 | 0 |
| 5 | 0 | 1 | 0 | 1 | 13 | 1 | 1 | 0 | 1 |
| 6 | 0 | 1 | 1 | 0 | 14 | 1 | 1 | 1 | 0 |
| 7 | 0 | 1 | 1 | 1 | 15 | 1 | 1 | 1 | 1 |

# Key for binary number cards

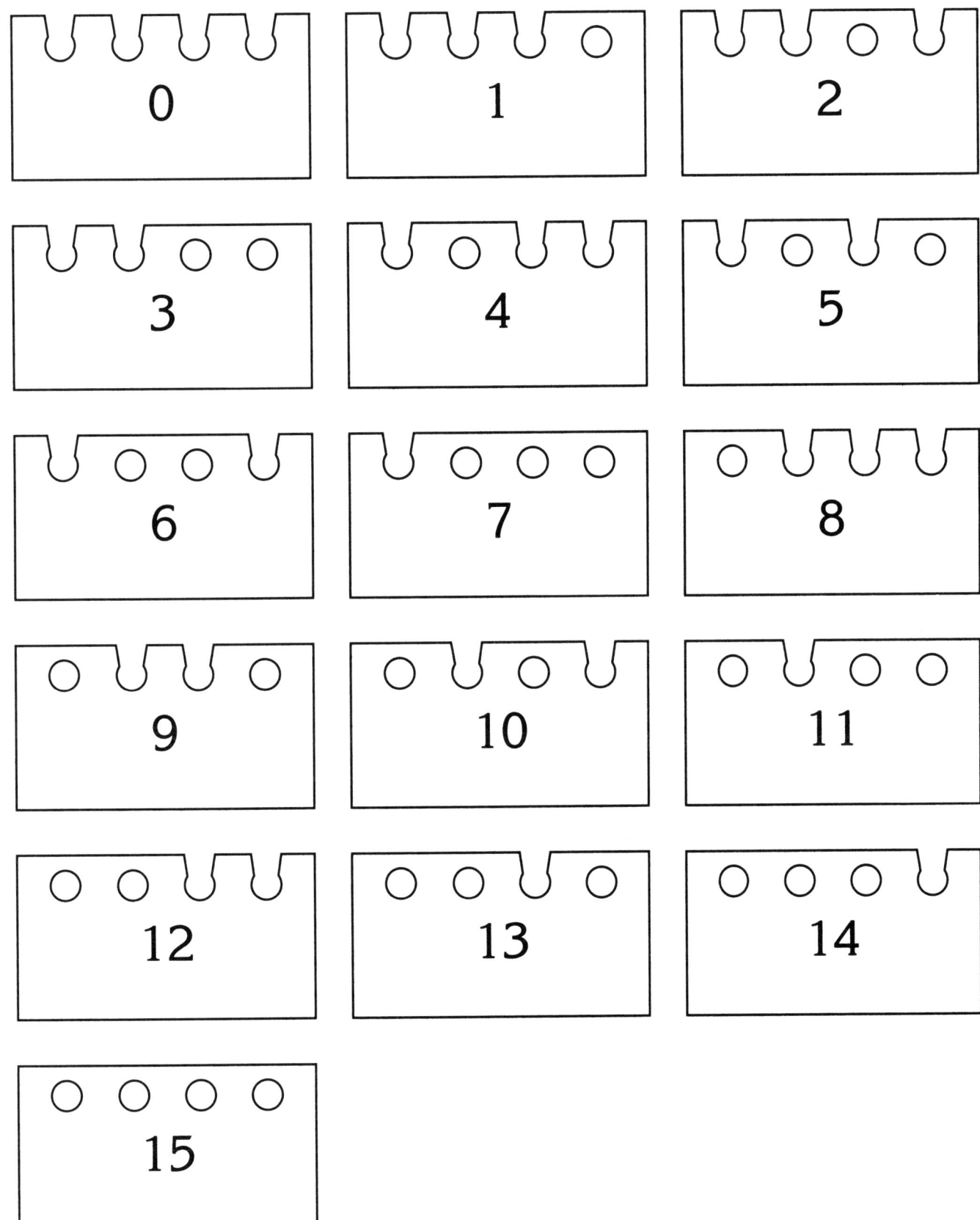

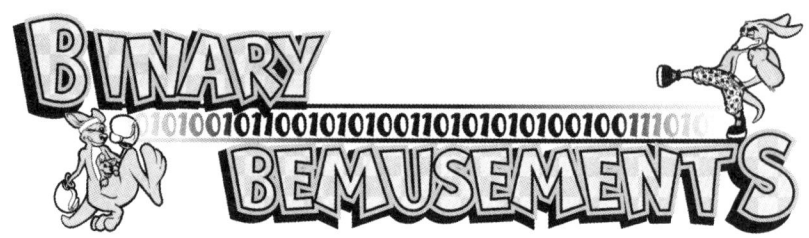

## Key Question

What are number bases, and how do our number cards—which are based on the binary system—work?

## Learning Goals

### Students will:

- expand their knowledge of the binary number system by creating and explaining binary number cards, and

- gain a basic understanding of other number bases.

# An Introduction to Number Bases

The numeration system that you use everyday is called a base-ten system because each place represents a power of 10. Look at the chart below to see how the base-ten system can be broken down.

| Base to the power | $10^3$ | $10^2$ | $10^1$ | $10^0$ |
|---|---|---|---|---|
| Value of the place | 1000 | 100 | 10 | 1 |
| Name of the place | One thousands place | One hundreds place | Tens place | Ones place |

For example, the number 4852 can be thought of as four groupings of 1000; eight groupings of 100; five groupings of 10; and two groupings of one. Therefore, it could also be written:
$4 \times 10^3 + 8 \times 10^2 + 5 \times 10^1 + 2 \times 10^0$.

In addition to the base-ten system that you are used to, there are many other number base systems, but all operate on the same principles as the base-ten system. In any base system, the first place represents the base to the zero power; the second place represents the base to the first power, and so on.

**b** = Any base

Therefore, in a base-five system, you would have the ones place, the fives place, the twenty-fives place, the one hundred twenty-fives place, and so on as shown in the chart below.

| Base to the power | $5^3$ | $5^2$ | $5^1$ | $5^0$ |
|---|---|---|---|---|
| Value of the place | 125 | 25 | 5 | 1 |
| Name of the place | One hundred twenty-fives place | Twenty-fives place | Fives place | Ones place |

In this activity, you will be working with a base-two system. Using what you have learned about base systems above, complete the chart below for a base-two system.

## Base Two

| Base to the power | | | | $2^0$ |
|---|---|---|---|---|
| Value of the place | | | | 1 |
| Name of the place | | | | Ones place |

JUST FOR THE FUN OF IT! BOOK TWO

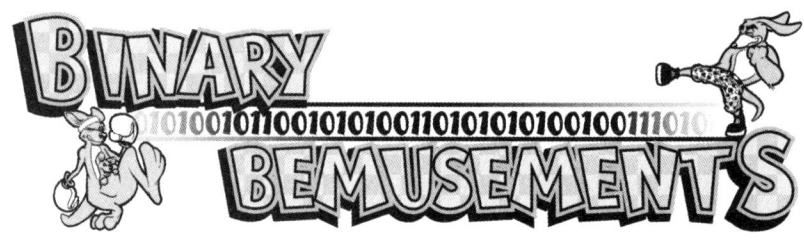

# Binary Bemusements

As you have already learned, the binary system is based on the powers of two. Using the first four powers of two, fill in the chart below by writing in all possible combinations in the appropriate spaces. For example, 1, 2, 4 is one possible three-number combination. Keep in mind that the order of the numbers does not matter—1, 2, 4 is the same as 2, 4, 1. In the total column, write the sum of the numbers (1 + 2 + 4 = 7).

$2^3 = $ _____      $2^2 = $ _____      $2^1 = $ _____      $2^0 = $ _____

| One-Number Combinations | Total |
|---|---|
|  |  |
|  |  |
|  |  |
|  |  |
| **Two-Number Combinations** |  |
|  |  |
|  |  |
|  |  |
|  |  |
|  |  |
|  |  |
| **Three-Number Combinations** |  |
| 4, 2, 1 | 7 |
|  |  |
|  |  |
| **Four-Number Combinations** |  |
|  |  |

JUST FOR THE FUN OF IT! BOOK TWO

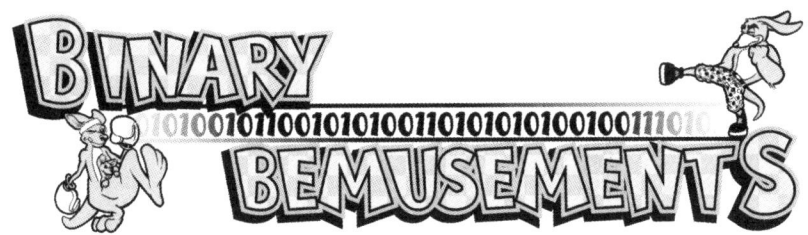

# Binary Bemusements

Now that you have discovered that it is possible to make all of the numbers from zero to 15 using the powers of two, you will learn how to write those numbers using the binary system. The binary system is a base-two system, which means that it uses only two digits—one and zero. The ones and zeroes in binary stand for the different powers of two, depending on their location. If there is a zero, it means that you do not count that power of two in the total. If there is a one, it means that you do count that power of two in your total. The number on the far right stands for $2^0$, and each number to the left of it stands for the next power of two. For example, to read the binary number 1011, you would add $2^3 + 0 + 2^1 + 2^0$, which is 11 in base ten. Using this information and the example given, fill in the table below, writing the numbers from zero to 15 in binary.

## The numbers from zero to 15 in binary

|  | $2^3$ | $2^2$ | $2^1$ | $2^0$ |  | $2^3$ | $2^2$ | $2^1$ | $2^0$ |
|---|---|---|---|---|---|---|---|---|---|
| 0 |  |  |  |  | 8 |  |  |  |  |
| 1 |  |  |  |  | 9 |  |  |  |  |
| 2 |  |  |  |  | 10 |  |  |  |  |
| 3 |  |  |  |  | 11 | 1 | 0 | 1 | 1 |
| 4 |  |  |  |  | 12 |  |  |  |  |
| 5 |  |  |  |  | 13 |  |  |  |  |
| 6 |  |  |  |  | 14 |  |  |  |  |
| 7 |  |  |  |  | 15 |  |  |  |  |

JUST FOR THE FUN OF IT! BOOK TWO  205  © 2010 AIMS Education Foundation

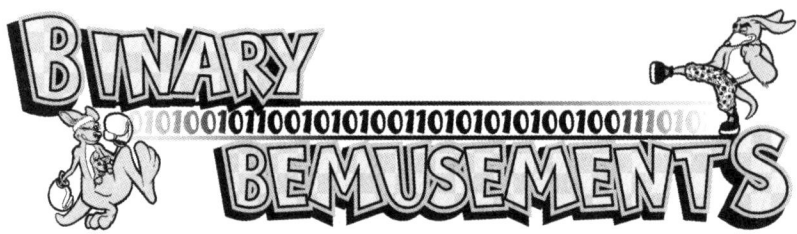

Now that you have written the numbers from zero to 15 in binary, you will be able to make your own set of binary cards. These cards, when used properly, will always put themselves in numerical order.

1. Your teacher has 16 cards for you. Take the cards and number them from zero to 15, making sure that the holes are at the top of the cards.
2. The holes in your cards represent ones. To make a zero, you must change a hole into a slot by cutting the top of the hole so that it is open to the edge of the card, as shown below.

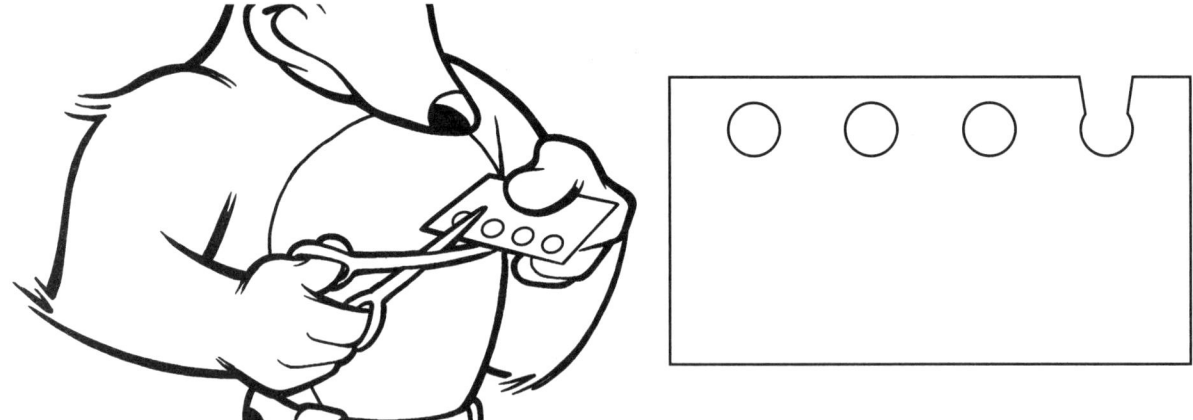

3. Using your binary chart from the previous page, cut the appropriate holes in each card so that the slots and holes show the same number in binary as you have written on the card. In the example below of the number 11, the third hole from the right has been cut into a slot because the number 11 in binary is 1011.

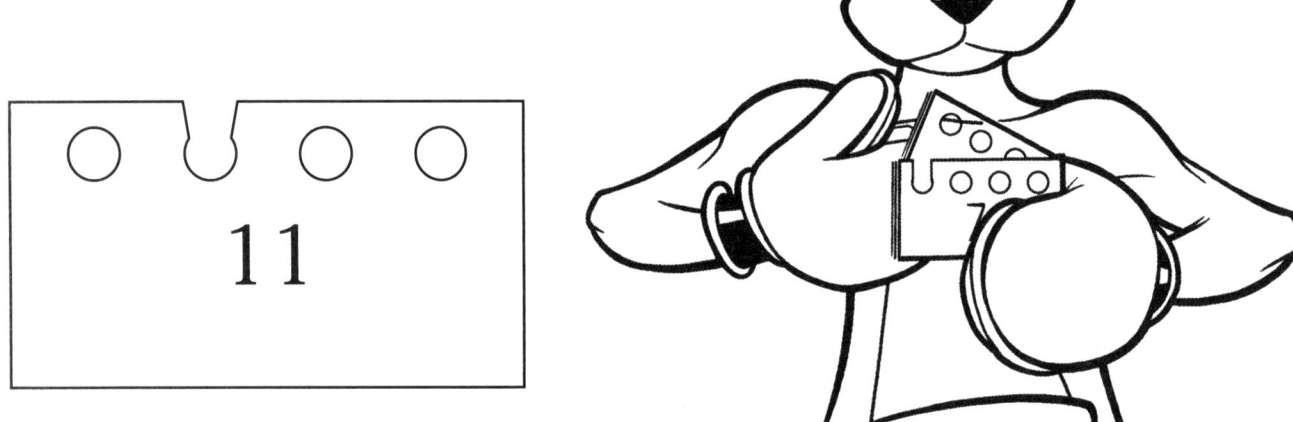

4. Once you have successfully done that, your binary cards are ready to work. First, mix up the cards so that they are not in any particular order, being sure to keep all of the holes/slots at the top of the cards. Then, take a straightened jumbo paper clip and insert it into the far right hole/slot. Pull up, separating the cards with holes in the first space from those with slots in the first space. Put the cards with holes (the ones on the paper clip) behind the other cards. Move the paper clip to the second hole/slot and repeat this process. When you have done this with the third and fourth holes/slots, your binary cards should once again be in order.

JUST FOR THE FUN OF IT! BOOK TWO © 2010 AIMS Education Foundation

1. Why do your binary cards put themselves in order when you follow the instructions properly?

2. What would happen if you started with the holes/slots on the left side of the card and moved to the right?

3. Why do you think this is?

4. What would happen if you put the cards that you separate each time in front of the rest of the cards instead behind?

5. Can you explain this?

6. What other interesting things have you discovered about your binary cards?

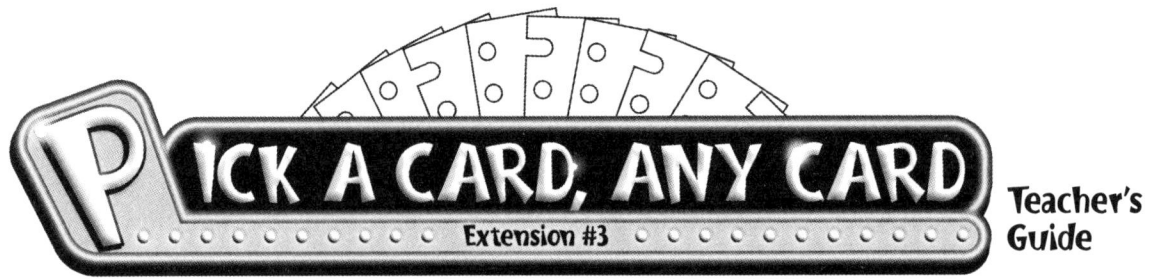

# Pick a Card, Any Card
## Extension #3
### Teacher's Guide

1. To introduce this extension, have a student pick a number between zero and 15. Using the same principle that you used to read students' minds in *Mind Reader's Magic Cards*, it is possible to "magically" pull any number a student picks from the stack of binary cards. The process is as follows:

    a. Mentally convert the chosen number into binary.

    b. Insert your paper clip into the spaces that correspond with ones in the number, one at a time. Put the cards that fall through aside—they cannot contain the number you are looking for (slots = zero).

    c. Insert your paper clip into the spaces that correspond to zeros in the number, one at a time. This time, discard whatever cards cling to the paper clip, since they also cannot be the number you are looking for (holes = one).

    d. If you have completed this process correctly, you should be left with one number card, and provided you made the correct conversion into binary, it should be the number you were trying to pull from the stack.

2. Hand out the student page and allow students time to discover the secret and practice its execution on their classmates.

3. If desired, have a time of class discussion to clarify the process and make sure that everyone understands the reason it works.

4. Encourage students to take their binary cards home and impress their family with their amazing mathematical magic.

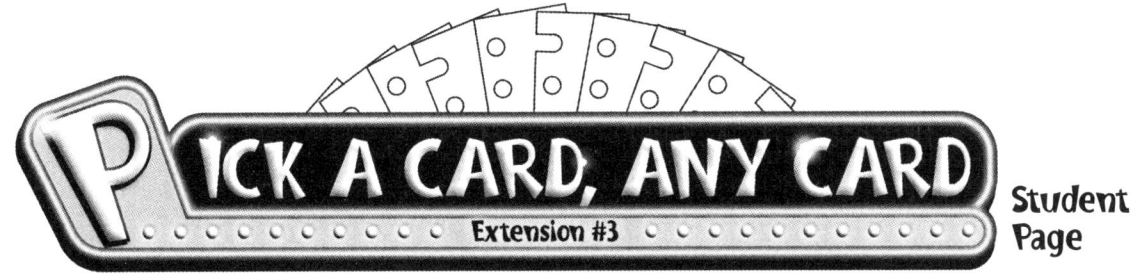
# Student Page

Your teacher has just shown you how it is possible to "magically" pull any single number from your stack of binary cards. Using what you have learned about binary numbers, try to replicate this process yourself. Once you have discovered the necessary technique, answer the questions below.

1. Describe the process you went through to pull one specific number from the stack.

2. How did this process change for different numbers?

3. Why is it possible to pull any number from zero to 15 from your stack of binary cards?

4. How would you pull the number 14 out if the holes were zeroes and the slots were ones, instead of the other way around?

**Challenge:**
Describe the process you would have to go through to pull the number 17 from a stack of binary cards that go from zero to 31 (17 in binary is 10001).

JUST FOR THE FUN OF IT! BOOK TWO

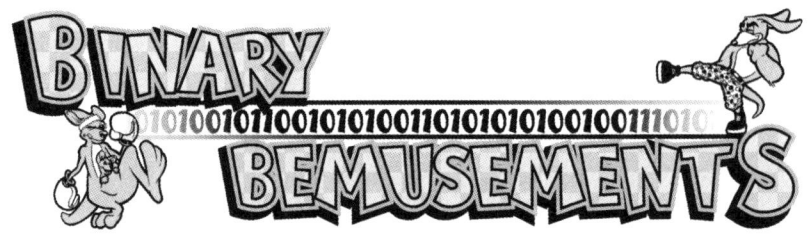

## Connecting Learning

1. What did you learn about the base-two system from this activity?

2. Why do your binary cards work?

3. Do you think you could make a binary card for the number 16?

4. How would it look?

5. Why do you have to move your pencil from right to left to put the cards in order?

6. What are you wondering now?

# The AIMS Program

AIMS is the acronym for "Activities Integrating Mathematics and Science." Such integration enriches learning and makes it meaningful and holistic. AIMS began as a project of Fresno Pacific University to integrate the study of mathematics and science in grades K-9, but has since expanded to include language arts, social studies, and other disciplines.

AIMS is a continuing program of the non-profit AIMS Education Foundation. It had its inception in a National Science Foundation funded program whose purpose was to explore the effectiveness of integrating mathematics and science. The project directors, in cooperation with 80 elementary classroom teachers, devoted two years to a thorough field-testing of the results and implications of integration.

The approach met with such positive results that the decision was made to launch a program to create instructional materials incorporating this concept. Despite the fact that thoughtful educators have long recommended an integrative approach, very little appropriate material was available in 1981 when the project began. A series of writing projects ensued, and today the AIMS Education Foundation is committed to continuing the creation of new integrated activities on a permanent basis.

The AIMS program is funded through the sale of books, products, and professional-development workshops, and through proceeds from the Foundation's endowment. All net income from programs and products flows into a trust fund administered by the AIMS Education Foundation. Use of these funds is restricted to support of research, development, and publication of new materials. Writers donate all their rights to the Foundation to support its ongoing program. No royalties are paid to the writers.

The rationale for integration lies in the fact that science, mathematics, language arts, social studies, etc., are integrally interwoven in the real world, from which it follows that they should be similarly treated in the classroom where students are being prepared to live in that world. Teachers who use the AIMS program give enthusiastic endorsement to the effectiveness of this approach.

Science encompasses the art of questioning, investigating, hypothesizing, discovering, and communicating. Mathematics is a language that provides clarity, objectivity, and understanding. The language arts provide us with powerful tools of communication. Many of the major contemporary societal issues stem from advancements in science and must be studied in the context of the social sciences. Therefore, it is timely that all of us take seriously a more holistic method of educating our students. This goal motivates all who are associated with the AIMS Program. We invite you to join us in this effort.

Meaningful integration of knowledge is a major recommendation coming from the nation's professional science and mathematics associations. The American Association for the Advancement of Science in *Science for All Americans* strongly recommends the integration of mathematics, science, and technology. The National Council of Teachers of Mathematics places strong emphasis on applications of mathematics found in science investigations. AIMS is fully aligned with these recommendations.

Extensive field testing of AIMS investigations confirms these beneficial results:

1. Mathematics becomes more meaningful, hence more useful, when it is applied to situations that interest students.
2. The extent to which science is studied and understood is increased when mathematics and science are integrated.
3. There is improved quality of learning and retention, supporting the thesis that learning which is meaningful and relevant is more effective.
4. Motivation and involvement are increased dramatically as students investigate real-world situations and participate actively in the process.

We invite you to become part of this classroom teacher movement by using an integrated approach to learning and sharing any suggestions you may have. The AIMS Program welcomes you!

# AIMS Education Foundation Programs

When you host an AIMS workshop for elementary and middle school educators, you will know your teachers are receiving effective, usable training they can apply in their classrooms immediately.

**AIMS Workshops are Designed for Teachers**
- Correlated to your state standards;
- Address key topic areas, including math content, science content, and process skills;
- Provide practice of activity-based teaching;
- Address classroom management issues and higher-order thinking skills;
- Give you AIMS resources; and
- Offer optional college (graduate-level) credits for many courses.

**AIMS Workshops Fit District/Administrative Needs**
- Flexible scheduling and grade-span options;
- Customized (one-, two-, or three-day) workshops meet specific schedule, topic, state standards, and grade-span needs;
- Prepackaged four-day workshops for in-depth math and science training available (includes all materials and expenses);
- Sustained staff development is available for which workshops can be scheduled throughout the school year;
- Eligible for funding under the Title I and Title II sections of No Child Left Behind; and
- Affordable professional development—consecutive-day workshops offer considerable savings.

**University Credit—Correspondence Courses**
AIMS offers correspondence courses through a partnership with Fresno Pacific University.
- Convenient distance-learning courses—you study at your own pace and schedule. No computer or Internet access required!

**Introducing AIMS State-Specific Science Curriculum**
Developed to meet 100% of your state's standards, AIMS' State-Specific Science Curriculum gives students the opportunity to build content knowledge, thinking skills, and fundamental science processes.
- Each grade-specific module has been developed to extend the AIMS approach to full-year science programs. Modules can be used as a complete curriculum or as a supplement to existing materials.
- Each standards-based module includes math, reading, hands-on investigations, and assessments.

Like all AIMS resources, these modules are able to serve students at all stages of readiness, making these a great value across the grades served in your school.

For current information regarding the programs described above, please complete the following form and mail it to: P.O. Box 8120, Fresno, CA 93747.

---

## Information Request

Please send current information on the items checked:

\_\_\_ *Basic Information Packet* on AIMS materials
\_\_\_ Hosting information for AIMS workshops
\_\_\_ AIMS State-Specific Science Curriculum

Name: _____

Phone: _____ E-mail: _____

Address: _____
       Street                       City                    State        Zip

**YOUR K-9 MATH AND SCIENCE CLASSROOM ACTIVITIES RESOURCE**

The AIMS Magazine is your source for standards-based, hands-on math and science investigations. Each issue is filled with teacher-friendly, ready-to-use activities that engage students in meaningful learning.

- *Four issues each year (fall, winter, spring, and summer).*

**Current issue is shipped with all past issues within that volume.**

| | | | |
|---|---|---|---|
| 1824 | Volume XXIV | 2009-2010 | $19.95 |
| 1825 | Volume XXV | 2010-2011 | $19.95 |

Two-Volume Combination

| | | | |
|---|---|---|---|
| M20810 | Volumes XXIII & XXIV | 2008-2010 | $34.95 |
| M20911 | Volumes XXIV & XXV | 2009-2011 | $34.95 |

**Complete volumes available for purchase:**

| | | | |
|---|---|---|---|
| 1802 | Volume II | 1987-1988 | $19.95 |
| 1804 | Volume IV | 1989-1990 | $19.95 |
| 1805 | Volume V | 1990-1991 | $19.95 |
| 1807 | Volume VII | 1992-1993 | $19.95 |
| 1808 | Volume VIII | 1993-1994 | $19.95 |
| 1809 | Volume IX | 1994-1995 | $19.95 |
| 1810 | Volume X | 1995-1996 | $19.95 |
| 1811 | Volume XI | 1996-1997 | $19.95 |
| 1812 | Volume XII | 1997-1998 | $19.95 |
| 1813 | Volume XIII | 1998-1999 | $19.95 |
| 1814 | Volume XIV | 1999-2000 | $19.95 |
| 1815 | Volume XV | 2000-2001 | $19.95 |
| 1816 | Volume XVI | 2001-2002 | $19.95 |
| 1817 | Volume XVII | 2002-2003 | $19.95 |
| 1818 | Volume XVIII | 2003-2004 | $19.95 |
| 1819 | Volume XIX | 2004-2005 | $19.95 |
| 1820 | Volume XX | 2005-2006 | $19.95 |
| 1821 | Volume XXI | 2006-2007 | $19.95 |
| 1822 | Volume XXII | 2007-2008 | $19.95 |
| 1823 | Volume XXIII | 2008-2009 | $19.95 |

Volumes II to XIX include 10 issues.

**Call 1.888.733.2467 or go to www.aimsedu.org**

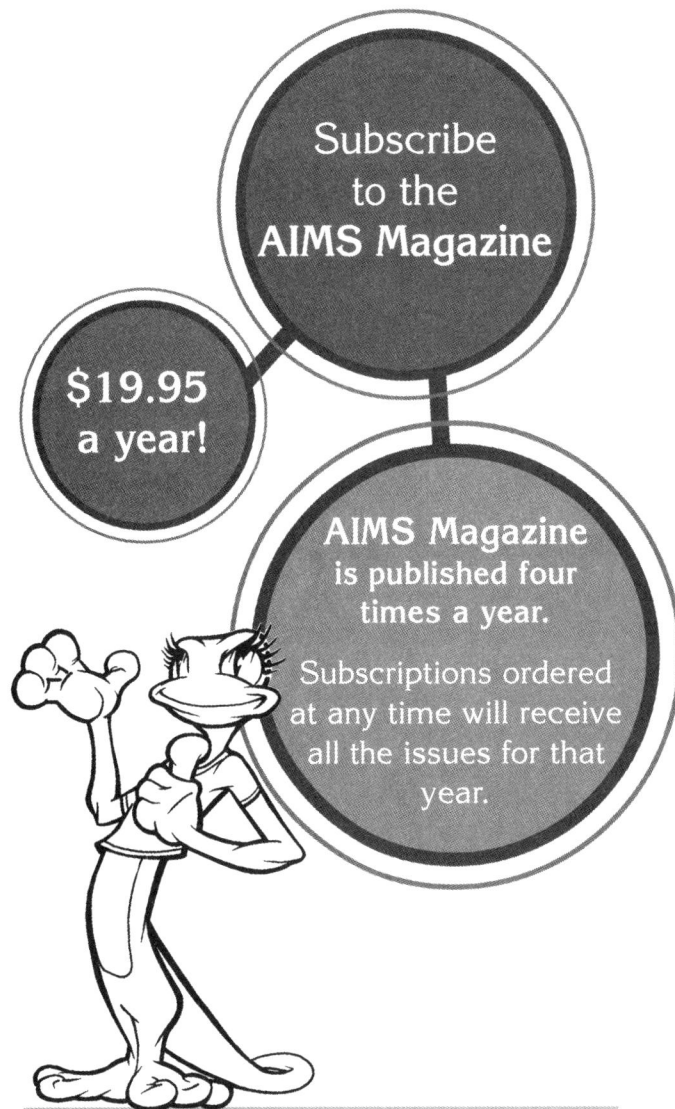

**Subscribe to the AIMS Magazine**

**$19.95 a year!**

AIMS Magazine is published four times a year. Subscriptions ordered at any time will receive all the issues for that year.

**AIMS Online—www.aimsedu.org**

To see all that AIMS has to offer, check us out on the Internet at www.aimsedu.org. At our website you can preview and purchase AIMS books and individual activities, learn about State-Specific Science and Essential Math, explore professional development workshops and online learning opportunities, search our activities database, buy manipulatives and other classroom resources, and download free resources including articles, puzzles, and sample AIMS activities.

**AIMS E-mail Specials**

While visiting the AIMS website, sign up for our FREE e-mail newsletter with monthly subscriber-only specials. You'll also receive advance notice of new products.

Sign up today!

# AIMS Program Publications

Actions With Fractions, 4-9
The Amazing Circle, 4-9
Awesome Addition and Super Subtraction, 2-3
Bats Incredible! 2-4
Brick Layers II, 4-9
The Budding Botanist, 3-6
Chemistry Matters, 4-7
Counting on Coins, K-2
Cycles of Knowing and Growing, 1-3
Crazy About Cotton, 3-7
Critters, 2-5
Earth Book, 6-9
Electrical Connections, 4-9
Exploring Environments, K-6
Fabulous Fractions, 3-6
Fall Into Math and Science*, K-1
Field Detectives, 3-6
Finding Your Bearings, 4-9
Floaters and Sinkers, 5-9
From Head to Toe, 5-9
Glide Into Winter With Math and Science*, K-1
Gravity Rules! 5-12
Hardhatting in a Geo-World, 3-5
Historical Connections in Mathematics, Vol. I, 5-9
Historical Connections in Mathematics, Vol. II, 5-9
Historical Connections in Mathematics, Vol. III, 5-9
It's About Time, K-2
It Must Be A Bird, Pre-K-2
Jaw Breakers and Heart Thumpers, 3-5
Looking at Geometry, 6-9
Looking at Lines, 6-9
Machine Shop, 5-9
Magnificent Microworld Adventures, 6-9
Marvelous Multiplication and Dazzling Division, 4-5
Math + Science, A Solution, 5-9
Mathematicians are People, Too
Mathematicians are People, Too, Vol. II
Mostly Magnets, 3-6
Movie Math Mania, 6-9
Multiplication the Algebra Way, 6-8
Out of This World, 4-8
Paper Square Geometry:
    The Mathematics of Origami, 5-12
Puzzle Play, 4-8
Pieces and Patterns*, 5-9
Popping With Power, 3-5
Positive vs. Negative, 6-9
Primarily Bears*, K-6
Primarily Earth, K-3
Primarily Magnets, K-2
Primarily Physics*, K-3
Primarily Plants, K-3
Primarily Weather, K-3
Problem Solving: Just for the Fun of It! 4-9
Problem Solving: Just for the Fun of It! Book Two, 4-9
Proportional Reasoning, 6-9
Ray's Reflections, 4-8
Sensational Springtime, K-2
Sense-Able Science, K-1
Shapes, Solids, and More: Concepts in Geometry, 2-3
The Sky's the Limit, 5-9
Soap Films and Bubbles, 4-9
Solve It! K-1: Problem-Solving Strategies, K-1
Solve It! 2nd: Problem-Solving Strategies, 2
Solve It! 3rd: Problem-Solving Strategies, 3
Solve It! 4th: Problem-Solving Strategies, 4
Solve It! 5th: Problem-Solving Strategies, 5
Solving Equations: A Conceptual Approach, 6-9
Spatial Visualization, 4-9
Spills and Ripples, 5-12
Spring Into Math and Science*, K-1
Statistics and Probability, 6-9
Through the Eyes of the Explorers, 5-9
Under Construction, K-2
Water, Precious Water, 4-6
Weather Sense: Temperature, Air Pressure, and Wind, 4-5
Weather Sense: Moisture, 4-5
What's Next, Volume 1, 4-12
What's Next, Volume 2, 4-12
What's Next, Volume 3, 4-12
Winter Wonders, K-2

### Essential Math
Area Formulas for Parallelograms, Triangles, and Trapezoids, 6-8
Circumference and Area of Circles, 5-7
Measurement of Prisms, Pyramids, Cylinders, and Cones, 6-8
Measurement of Rectangular Solids, 5-7
Perimeter and Area of Rectangles, 4-6
The Pythagorean Relationship, 6-8

### Spanish Edition
Constructores II: Ingeniería Creativa Con Construcciones
    LEGO®, 4-9
    The entire book is written in Spanish. English pages not included.

* Spanish supplements are available for these books. They are only available as downloads from the AIMS website. The supplements contain only the student pages in Spanish; you will need the English version of the book for the teacher's text.

For further information, contact:
AIMS Education Foundation • P.O. Box 8120 • Fresno, California 93747-8120
www.aimsedu.org • 559.255.6396 (fax) • 888.733.2467 (toll free)

# Duplication Rights

No part of any AIMS books, magazines, activities, or content—digital or otherwise—may be reproduced or transmitted in any form or by any means—including photocopying, taping, or information storage/retrieval systems—except as noted below.

## Standard Duplication Rights

- A person or school purchasing AIMS activities (in books, magazines, or in digital form) is hereby granted permission to make up to 200 copies of any portion of those activities, provided these copies will be used for educational purposes and only at one school site.
- Workshop or conference presenters may make one copy of any portion of a purchased activity for each participant, with a limit of five activities per workshop or conference session.
- All copies must bear the AIMS Education Foundation copyright information.

Standard duplication rights apply to activities received at workshops, free sample activities provided by AIMS, and activities received by conference participants.

## Unlimited Duplication Rights

Unlimited duplication rights may be purchased in cases where AIMS users wish to:
- make more than 200 copies of a book/magazine/activity,
- use a book/magazine/activity at more than one school site, or
- make an activity available on the Internet (see below).

These rights permit unlimited duplication of purchased books, magazines, and/or activities (including revisions) for use at a given school site.

Activities received at workshops are eligible for upgrade from standard to unlimited duplication rights.

Free sample activities and activities received as a conference participant are not eligible for upgrade from standard to unlimited duplication rights.

State-Specific Science modules are licensed to one classroom/one teacher and are therefore not eligible for upgrade from standard to unlimited duplication rights.

## Upgrade Fees

The fees for upgrading from standard to unlimited duplication rights are:
- $5 per activity per site,
- $25 per book per site, and
- $10 per magazine issue per site.

The cost of upgrading is shown in the following examples:
- activity: 5 activities x 5 sites x $5 = $125
- book: 10 books x 5 sites x $25 = $1250
- magazine issue: 1 issue x 5 sites x $10 = $50

## Purchasing Unlimited Duplication Rights

To purchase unlimited duplication rights, please provide us the following:
1. The name of the individual responsible for coordinating the purchase of duplication rights.
2. The title of each book, activity, and magazine issue to be covered.
3. The number of school sites and name of each site for which rights are being purchased.
4. Payment (check, purchase order, credit card)

Requested duplication rights are automatically authorized with payment. The individual responsible for coordinating the purchase of duplication rights will be sent a certificate verifying the purchase.

## Internet Use

AIMS materials may be made available on the Internet if all of the following stipulations are met:
1. The materials to be put online are purchased as PDF files from AIMS (i.e., no scanned copies).
2. Unlimited duplication rights are purchased for all materials to be put online for each school at which they will be used. (See above.)
3. The materials are made available via a secure, password-protected system that can only be accessed by employees at schools for which duplication rights have been purchased.

AIMS materials may not be made available on any publicly accessible Internet site.